100 GUMBO RECIPES

THE BEST MIX FOR GUMBO

Mya Hale

Disclaimer

The information contained in this eBook is meant to serve as a comprehensive collection of strategies that the author of this eBook has done research about. Summaries, strategies, tips, and tricks are only recommended by the author, and reading this eBook will not guarantee that one's results will exactly mirror the author's results. The author of the eBook has made all reasonable efforts to provide current and accurate information for the readers of the eBook. The author and its associates will not be held liable for any unintentional error or omissions that may be found. The material in the eBook may include information from third parties. Third-party materials comprise opinions expressed by their owners. As such, the author of the eBook does not assume responsibility or liability for any third-party material or opinions. Whether because of the progression of the internet, or the unforeseen changes in company policy and editorial submission guidelines, what is stated as fact at the time of this writing may become outdated or inapplicable later.

TABLE OF CONTENTS

INTRODUCTION

Gumbo is the essence of Creole and Cajun cooking, the mandatory dish on every restaurant menu and the heart of home cooking. It showcases the best indigenous shellfish as well as local sausages, poultry, wild game, and spices. It originated in Louisiana in the eighteenth century and derives its name from either the Bantu word for okra (gombo) or the Choctaw word for filé (kombo). Both okra and filé, which is ground sassafras leaves used by Native Americans, serve as thickeners for gumbo, along with the roux, a base of flour browned in oil. The most common thickener is the roux, which is similar to gravy. The extent to which it is browned determines the color of the gumbo. Local cooks often take it to a dark-brown color that gives the finished product a deep and robust flavor. Traditionally, onions, celery, and bell pepper (known as the trinity of local cooking) plus garlic are sizzled in the roux, and stock is added to make a Gumbo. Ingredients ranging from shellfish to poultry to wild game create the type and taste of the gumbo. Seasonings such as cayenne pepper, thyme, and bay leaf alter the flavor of the dish to please the cook, and the gumbo is served in bowls over rice.

The most distinctive styles of gumbo are Creole (New Orleans) and Cajun (southwestern Louisiana). Creole uses tomatoes, and Cajun does not. Therefore, one is brown and the other is a reddish brown. Creole gumbo tends to have a thinner base, while a Cajun gumbo is heartier, darker and sometimes thicker, and is more apt to use game such as wild ducks. In south Louisiana, gumbos are served on all tables, rich or poor, and in most restaurants, upscale or otherwise.

BASE RECIPES

1. Roux

MAKES ABOUT 1 CUP

INGREDIENTS

1/2 cup vegetable oil

1/2 cup all-purpose flour

DIRECTIONS

Heat the oil in a large, heavy pot over high heat; add the flour and stir constantly until the mixture begins to brown. Reduce the heat to medium or medium-low and cook, stirring constantly, until the roux is medium-brown, or the color of peanut butter or milk chocolate.

If you prefer a darker gumbo, continue browning until the roux turns a dark-chocolate color. The darker the roux, the thinner the gumbo will be. Do not burn the roux, or it will ruin the taste of the gumbo. If it smells burnt, it has cooked too long. Most gumbos are tasty and slightly thick when the roux is the color of milk chocolate.

2. Seafood Stock

MAKES 5 CUPS

INGREDIENTS

1 1/2 pounds shells from shrimp, crawfish, or crabs

DIRECTIONS

Place shells in a medium pot and cover with cold water. Bring to a boil. Cover, reduce heat to medium-low and simmer for 30 minutes. Strain.

3. Poultry Stock

MAKES 8 CUPS

INGREDIENTS

3 pounds chicken, turkey, or duck bones

1 large onion, peeled and quartered

2 celery stalks, halved

2 carrots, quartered

1/2 tablespoon black peppercorns

2 large garlic cloves, halved

10 cups cold water

DIRECTIONS

Place all the Ingredients in a 6-quart pot. Bring to a boil. Reduce the heat to medium-low, cover the pot with the lid askew, and simmer for 2 1/2 hours. When cool enough to handle, strain. Cool completely and skim the fat from the top. If making ahead, chill in the refrigerator and skim off the solid fat.

4. Rice

MAKES 6-8 SERVINGS

INGREDIENTS

2 cups water

2 cups enriched long-grain rice

1/2 teaspoon salt

DIRECTIONS

In a small pot with a cover, bring the water to a boil. Add the rice and salt. Reduce the heat, cover, and simmer on the lowest heat until the water is absorbed, about 20 minutes. No stirring is necessary.

5. Creole Seasoning

MAKES 2 1/2 OUNCES

INGREDIENTS

2 tablespoons salt

2 teaspoons cayenne pepper

4 teaspoons freshly ground black pepper

4 teaspoons garlic powder

4 teaspoons paprika, sweet or hot, or to taste

4 teaspoons celery salt

2 teaspoons chili powder

DIRECTIONS

Whisk together all the Ingredients in a medium bowl. Store in a cleaned 2 1/2-ounce spice bottle. The seasoning will keep its strength for several months.

GUMBO RECIPES

6. Chicken and Shrimp Gumbo

SERVES 4

INGREDIENTS

2 tablespoons canola oil

¼ cup all-purpose flour

1 medium onion, diced

1 green bell pepper, seeded and diced

2 stalks celery, diced

3 garlic cloves, minced

1 tablespoon minced fresh thyme

¼ to ½ teaspoon cayenne pepper

½ cup dry white wine

1 (14-ounce) can no-salt-added diced tomatoes

2 cups water

1 (10-ounce) package frozen sliced okra

4 ounces smoked andouille sausage, diced

1-pound medium shrimp, peeled and deveined

1½ pounds cooked chicken breast, diced

DIRECTIONS

Heat the oil in a large stockpot or Dutch oven over medium-high heat. Add the flour and cook, whisking constantly.

Add the onion, bell pepper, celery, and garlic and cook, stirring occasionally, until the onions are soft, about 5 minutes.

Add the thyme and cayenne and cook for 1 minute more. Stir in the wine and bring to a boil, stirring occasionally.

Add the tomatoes with their juice, water, and okra and simmer, uncovered, for about 15 minutes. Add the sausage and shrimp, and simmer for about 5 minutes more.

Stir in the cooked chicken and continue to simmer, stirring occasionally, until the chicken is heated through and the shrimp is opaque.

7. Okra Chicken Gumbo

INGREDIENTS

- 1-pound medium shrimp peeled
- 1/2 pound skinless, boneless chicken breasts
- 1/2 cup coconut oil
- 3/4 cup almond flour
- 2 cups chopped onions
- 1 cup chopped celery
- 1 cup chopped green pepper
- 1 teaspoons ground cumin
- 1 Tablespoons minced fresh garlic
- 1 teaspoon fresh thyme chopped
- 1/2 teaspoons red pepper
- 6 cups chicken broth
- 2 cups diced tomatoes
- 3 cups sliced okra
- 1/2 cup fresh parsley chopped
- 2 bay leaves
- 1 teaspoon hot sauce

DIRECTIONS

a) Sauté' chicken on high heat until brown in a large pot. Remove and set aside. Chop onions, celery, and green pepper and set aside.

b) Place oil and flour in pot. Stir well and brown to make a roux. When roux is done add chopped vegetables. Sauté on low heat for 10 minutes.

c) Slowly add chicken broth stirring constantly.

d) Add chicken and all other ingredients except the okra, shrimp and parsley, which will be saved for the end.

e) Cover and simmer on low for half an hour. Remove lid and cook for half an hour more, stirring occasionally.

f) Add shrimp, okra and parsley. Continue to cook on low heat uncovered for 15 minutes.

8. Dutch Oven Scallop gumbo

TOTAL COOKING TIME: 36 MINUTES
SERVINGS: 4
EQUIPMENT: 12-INCH DUTCH OVEN

INGREDIENTS

2 pounds of baby scallops
3 tablespoons of flour
2 onions, chopped
2 bell peppers, chopped
1/2 cups celery, chopped
2-pound okra, sliced
4 tablespoons cooking oil
3 tomatoes, sliced
Minced Garlic, 2 cloves
Pinch salt, and pepper

DIRECTIONS

Make a roux using flour and cooking oil.
Add the bell pepper, onion, and garlic along with water, salt, and pepper.
Add the celery, okra, and tomato and cook for 30 minutes with the cover on.
Add Scallops and simmer for 6 more minutes.

9. Dutch Oven chicken gumbo

TOTAL COOKING TIME: 15 MINUTES
SERVINGS: 6
EQUIPMENT: 12-INCH DUTCH OVEN

INGREDIENTS

2 tablespoons of cooking oil
1 cups celery, chopped
2-pound okra, sliced
Minced Garlic, 2 cloves
3 tomatoes, sliced
2 Tablespoons flour
2 pounds of chicken breasts, cubed
Salt and pepper
2 bell peppers, chopped
2 onions, chopped

DIRECTIONS

Make a roux using flour and cooking oil. Cook while frequently tossing until browned.
Add the bell pepper, onion, and garlic along with water, salt, and pepper.
Add the celery, okra, and tomato.
After adding the chicken, cook for another 6 minutes.

10. Dutch Oven duck gumbo

TOTAL COOKING TIME: 2 HOURS 20 MINUTES
SERVINGS: 12
EQUIPMENT: 12-INCH DUTCH OVEN

INGREDIENTS
DUCK:
2 bay leaves
3 teaspoons salt
3 ducks
2 ribs of celery
1 gallon of water
1 onion, quartered
1 teaspoon Pepper
2 carrots
GUMBO:
1 cup oil
¼ cup chopped parsley
1 cup flour
Minced Garlic, 2 cloves
½ cup celery, chopped
1 cup bell pepper, diced
2 cups of cooked rice
1 point oysters and liquor
1-pound okra, sliced
1 cup onion, diced
4 tablespoons bacon fat
1 pound raw and peeled shrimp

DIRECTIONS:

DUCK

Cook duck, onion, bay leaves, celery, salt, and pepper for roughly 1 hour.

FOR GUMBO:

Mix flour and oil using a Dutch oven.

Add garlic, onion, celery, and green pepper; sauté okra in bacon fat for 20 minutes.

Heat the broth in a Gumbo pot before adding the roux and vegetable mixture.

Cook for 1 hour, covered, with the okra.

Add the shrimp, oysters, and liqueur.

11. Gulf Coast Gumbo

MAKES 8 SERVINGS

INGREDIENTS

1 cup vegetable oil

1 1/2 cups all-purpose flour

2 1/2 cups chopped onion

1 1/2 cups chopped celery

1 1/2 cups chopped green bell pepper

3 tablespoons chopped garlic

1 teaspoon Emeril's Original Essence or other Creole seasoning

1 1/2 teaspoons salt

1 teaspoon freshly ground black pepper

1/2 teaspoon cayenne pepper

2 bay leaves

1 teaspoon dried thyme

1 teaspoon dried oregano

1 pound smoked sausage, cut into 1/2-inch-thick rounds

1 pound gumbo crabs, halved (see Note)

10 cups shrimp stock or water

1 pound cooked Louisiana crawfish tails, with any fat

1 pound peeled and deveined Gulf shrimp

1/2 cup chopped green onions, plus more for serving

1/4 cup chopped fresh parsley leaves, plus more for serving

Steamed white rice, for serving

DIRECTIONS

Heat a large Dutch oven or heavy-bottomed Gumbo pot over high heat for 1 minute. Carefully add the oil and then whisk in the flour. Reduce the heat to medium-high and stir the flour constantly, scraping every bit of the pan bottom, until the roux is evenly browned and the color of dark peanut butter, about 15 minutes. If the flour begins to color too fast, reduce the heat to medium. It is important to watch the roux and cook carefully to avoid burning it. Once the desired color is reached, add the onion, celery, bell pepper, garlic, Essence, salt, pepper, cayenne, bay leaves, thyme, oregano, and sausage. Continue to cook 5-7 minutes longer, or until the vegetables have softened.

Add the crabs and stock to the Dutch oven and bring to a boil. Reduce the heat to a steady simmer and cook until the flavors have come together and the sauce is velvety and smooth, about 2 hours, adding additional stock or water if the gumbo becomes too thick during cooking. The thickness of a gumbo is a matter of personal taste. Some folks like a very thick gumbo, while others prefer a thin, brothy gumbo. Add the amount of liquid to suit your preference.

When the gumbo is flavorful and just the right thickness, stir in the crawfish and shrimp and cook just until the shrimp are cooked through, 2-3 minutes longer. Stir in the green onions and parsley. Taste and adjust the seasoning, if necessary.

Serve the gumbo over bowls of steamed rice with additional chopped parsley and green onions as desired.

12. Chicken, Shrimp, and Tasso Gumbo

MAKES 6-8 SERVINGS

INGREDIENTS

4 boneless chicken thighs, cut into 2-inches pieces with the skin on

2 teaspoons kosher salt

1/2 teaspoon paprika

1/2 teaspoon freshly ground black pepper

1 1/2 cups vegetable oil

2 1/4 cups all-purpose flour, divided

1 pound diced tasso

1 medium onion, small diced

2 poblano peppers, small diced

1 small jalapeño, small diced

3 celery stalks, diced

4 garlic cloves, minced

2-3 teaspoons kosher salt (add 2, taste, and add the other if needed)

1 1/2 teaspoons freshly ground black pepper

1 teaspoon cayenne pepper

1 teaspoon paprika

1 teaspoon dried thyme

1 teaspoon filé powder

6 bay leaves

1 gallon chicken stock (or half shrimp stock and half chicken stock)

1 pound peeled Louisiana shrimp

Season the chicken with the salt, paprika, and pepper.

DIRECTIONS

Heat the oil in a 2-gallon heavy-bottomed pot to medium-high heat; the oil should gently sizzle when it is ready.

Coat the chicken with 1/2 cup of the flour and fry on both sides in the oil until light golden brown, then remove to a paper towel. It does not have to be cooked through at this point. Add any excess flour from seasoning the chicken to the remaining flour and add it to the oil. Stir over medium heat for about 40 minutes, or until the roux turns a deep reddish brown, but not too dark.

After the roux reaches the right color, add the tasso, the vegetables, and all the spices (reserving that little bit of salt, because some tasso is spicier than others) and cook for about 4 minutes.

Whisk in the stock and bring to a simmer, being sure to stir the bottom of the pot as the gumbo comes to a simmer so it doesn't stick. Simmer for about 30 minutes while skimming all the fat that rises to the surface.

Add the cooked chicken and shrimp at this point and simmer for another 45 minutes, still skimming any fat that floats to the top.

Serve immediately or the next day with some steamed rice and a side of creamy potato salad. Chef Link says, "I like to dip my potato salad in the gumbo."

13. Creole Gumbo

MAKES 8-10 SERVINGS

INGREDIENTS

1/2 pound chaurice, cut into bite-size pieces

1/2 pound smoked sausage, cut into bite-size pieces

1/2 pound beef stew meat

1/2 pound chicken gizzards, chopped

1 pound gumbo crabs

1/2 cup vegetable oil

1/2 cup all-purpose flour

2 large onions, chopped

3 quarts water, or more as desired

8 chicken wings, cut at joints and tips discarded

1/2 pound smoked ham, cut into 1/2-inch pieces

1 tablespoon paprika

1 teaspoon dried thyme

1 teaspoon salt

3 garlic cloves, minced

1 pound medium shrimp, peeled and deveined

2 dozen shucked oysters with their liquor

1/4 cup chopped fresh flat-leaf parsley

1 tablespoon filé powder

Cooked long-grain white rice, for serving

DIRECTIONS

Place the sausages, beef, gizzards, and crabs in a large, heavy pot. Cover and cook over medium heat for 30 minutes, stirring occasionally. You won't need extra fat, as the meat will render enough for cooking.

While the meats are cooking, make a roux: heat the oil in a skillet, add the flour, and stir constantly over medium heat until the roux is smooth and dark-brown in color. Add the onions and cook over low heat until soft. Empty the contents of the skillet into the pot holding the meat, mixing well. Slowly stir in the water and bring it to a boil. Add the chicken wings, ham, paprika, thyme, salt, and garlic, stir gently, and turn down the heat; cover and simmer for 45 minutes. If you prefer a thinner gumbo, add more water now.

Add the shrimp and oysters and cook several more minutes—watch for the shrimp to turn just pink and the oysters to curl—any more than that, and they will become tough. Remove the pot from the heat, stir in the parsley and filé powder, and enjoy in bowls over hot rice.

14. Creole Seafood Gumbo

MAKES 6-8 SERVINGS

INGREDIENTS

6 medium blue crabs or frozen gumbo crabs, thawed

2 1/2 pounds shrimp in shells with heads

2 dozen medium-to-large shucked oysters with their liquor

1 cup plus 1 tablespoon canola or other vegetable oil, divided

2 cups sliced okra, fresh or frozen and thawed

1 cup all-purpose flour

1 large onion, chopped

1 bunch green onions, chopped, white and green parts separated

1 green bell pepper, chopped

2 celery stalks, chopped

4 large garlic cloves, minced

2 large fresh tomatoes in season, peeled and chopped, or 1 (16-ounce) canned diced tomatoes with juice

3 bay leaves

1 teaspoon Italian seasoning

Salt, freshly ground black pepper, and Creole seasoning, to taste

1/4 cup minced flat-leaf parsley

Cooked long-grain white rice, for serving

DIRECTIONS

Prepare the crabs as described in "Preparing Crabs," page 23.

De-head, peel, and devein the shrimp, placing the heads and shells in a medium pot. Add enough water to cover the shells by at least 2 inches and bring to a boil. Cover, reduce the heat to low, and simmer for 30 minutes. When slightly cooled, strain the stock into a large measuring cup and discard the shells.

Strain the oysters and add the liquor to the shrimp stock. Add enough water to make 7 or 8 cups of liquid at this point (depending on how thick you like your gumbo). Check the oysters for shell fragments.

Heat 1 tablespoon of the oil in a wide skillet (not nonstick) and add the okra. Sauté over medium heat, stirring occasionally, until all stickiness disappears, about 15 minutes. Remove from heat.

Heat the remaining oil in a large, heavy pot over high heat; add the flour and stir constantly until the roux begins to brown. Reduce the heat to medium or medium-low and cook, stirring constantly, until the roux is the color of dark chocolate.

Add the onions, the white parts of the green onions, the bell pepper, and the celery and cook, stirring, until translucent. Add the garlic and cook a minute more. Add the tomatoes and the oyster liquor, shrimp stock, and water combination until a slightly thickened and smooth consistency is achieved.

Add the okra, crabs, bay leaves, and Italian seasoning and season with salt, pepper, and Creole seasoning; cover and simmer for 40 minutes.

Add the shrimp and simmer for 5 more minutes. Add the oysters and simmer until they curl, about 3 minutes.

Turn off the heat, remove the bay leaves, and stir in most of the green onion tops and parsley, leaving some for garnish. Serve in bowls over the rice. Add pieces of the crab to each bowl and garnish with onion tops and parsley. Offer crab or nut crackers for the legs.

15. Chicken and Andouille Gumbo

MAKES 6-8 SERVINGS

INGREDIENTS

2 pounds boneless chicken thighs, cut into bite-size chunks, or 1 whole chicken, cut into pieces

1 pound andouille sausage, cut into bite-size pieces

2 tablespoons plus 1/2 cup vegetable oil, divided

3/4 cup all-purpose flour

1 large onion, chopped

1 bunch green onions, chopped, white and green parts separated

1 green bell pepper, chopped

2 celery stalks, chopped

4 garlic cloves, minced

6 cups chicken stock

2 bay leaves

1 teaspoon Creole seasoning

Salt and freshly ground black pepper, to taste

1/3 cup chopped flat-leaf parsley

Cooked long-grain white rice, for serving

In a large, heavy pot, brown the chicken and andouille in 2 tablespoons of the oil. Remove the meat from the pot and set aside.

Add the remaining oil and the flour to the pot and stir constantly over high heat until the roux begins to brown. Reduce the heat to medium or medium-low and cook, stirring constantly, until the roux is the color of dark chocolate.

Add the onions, the white parts of the green onions, the bell pepper, the celery, and the garlic and sauté over low heat for about 5 minutes. Gradually stir in the chicken stock. Add the bay leaves and Creole seasoning and season with salt and pepper; cover and cook for about 45 minutes to 1 hour.

Add the green onion tops and parsley and remove the bay leaves. Serve in bowls over the rice with hot sauce and hot French bread.

16. Shrimp and Okra Gumbo

MAKES 8 SERVINGS

INGREDIENTS

3 pounds small-to-medium shrimp in shells with heads or 1 1/2 pounds peeled and deveined frozen shrimp, thawed

1 pound fresh okra, cut into 1/4-inch pieces, or frozen cut okra, thawed

1 tablespoon plus 1/2 cup vegetable oil, divided

1/2 cup all-purpose flour

1 large onion, chopped

1 bunch green onions, chopped, white and green parts separated

1 green bell pepper, chopped

2 celery stalks, chopped

3 large garlic cloves, minced

1 (14.5-ounce) can diced tomatoes

2 quarts shrimp stock or water

1 1/2 teaspoons Creole seasoning

2 bay leaves

1/2 teaspoon dried thyme

1/4 cup chopped flat-leaf parsley

Cooked long-grain white rice, for serving

French bread

If using fresh shrimp, de-head, peel, and devein them, placing the shells and heads in a medium pot. Add enough water to cover the shells by at least 2 inches and bring to a boil. Cover, reduce the heat to low, and simmer for 30 minutes. When slightly cooled, strain the stock into a large measuring cup and discard the shells.

If using fresh okra, heat 1 tablespoon of the oil in a medium-to-large skillet. Over medium heat, cook the okra, stirring occasionally, until the stringy liquid disappears. Set aside.

Heat the remaining oil in a large, heavy pot over high heat. Add the flour and stir constantly until the roux begins to brown. Reduce the heat to medium and cook, stirring constantly, until the roux is the color of milk chocolate. Add the onions and the white parts of the green onions and cook, stirring, until the onions begin to caramelize. Add the bell pepper and celery and cook until wilted. Add the garlic and cook a minute more.

Add the tomatoes and gradually stir in the stock or water. Add all the seasonings except the parsley, reduce the heat to low, cover, and simmer for 30 minutes. Add the shrimp and simmer until the shrimp turn pink, about 10 minutes. Remove from heat and add green onion tops and parsley and remove the bay leaves.

Serve in bowls over hot rice with hot French bread.

17. Super Gumbo

MAKES 10-12 SERVINGS

INGREDIENTS

2 pounds shrimp in shells with heads

1 pound fresh or frozen gumbo crabs, thawed if frozen

6 pieces chicken (such as legs and thighs)

Salt, pepper, and Creole seasoning, to taste

1 pound fresh okra, cut into pieces, or frozen cut okra, thawed

1 tablespoon plus 1 cup vegetable oil, divided

1 cup all-purpose flour

1 large onion, chopped

1 bunch green onions, chopped, white and green parts separated

1 green bell pepper, chopped

2 celery stalks, chopped

4 garlic cloves, minced

1/2 pound andouille or other smoked sausage, cut in quarters lengthwise and sliced 1/4 inch thick

2 fresh tomatoes, diced, or 1 (14.5-ounce) can diced tomatoes

2 tablespoons tomato paste

9 cups seafood or chicken stock, or a combination of the two

3 bay leaves

1/2 teaspoon Creole seasoning

1 teaspoon salt

Several turns on a black pepper mill

2 tablespoons chopped flat-leaf parsley

Cooked long-grain white rice, for serving

De-head, peel, and devein the shrimp, placing the heads and shells in a medium pot. Add enough water to cover the shells by at least 2 inches and bring to a boil. Cover, reduce the heat, and simmer for 30 minutes. When slightly cooled, strain the stock into a large measuring cup and discard the shells.

Remove anything other than the shells containing the crabmeat from the crabs, leaving the legs on and the yellow and orange fat in place. If any parts of the shell need cleaning, do so with a sponge.

Rinse and dry the chicken pieces and sprinkle liberally with salt, pepper, and Creole seasoning.

In a medium skillet, heat 1 tablespoon of the vegetable oil; add the okra and cook over high heat, stirring frequently, until it begins to brown slightly. Reduce the heat to medium and continue cooking until the sticky liquid disappears.

In a large, heavy pot heat 2 tablespoons of the remaining oil and brown the chicken pieces on all sides. Remove the chicken and set aside.

Add the remaining oil and the flour to the pot and stir over high heat until the roux turns light brown. Reduce the heat to medium and cook, stirring constantly, until the roux is dark brown (the color of peanut butter or slightly darker). Be careful not to burn it.

Add the onions, the white parts of the green onions, the bell pepper, and the celery and cook, stirring, until translucent. Add the garlic and cook a minute more. Add the sausage, tomatoes, and tomato paste and cook another 5 minutes. Gradually stir in the stock.

Add all the seasonings except the parsley. Bring to a boil, then reduce the heat to a simmer. Cover and cook for about 1 hour and 20 minutes, stirring occasionally and skimming the fat off the top. Add the shrimp, parsley, and green onion tops, turn up the heat and cook for several minutes until the shrimp turn pink. Taste to adjust the seasonings and remove the bay leaves.

Serve in bowls over the cooked rice.

18. Cajun Hen Gumbo

MAKES 6-8 SERVINGS

INGREDIENTS

1 (5- to 6-pound) hen

Salt, freshly ground black pepper, and cayenne pepper, to taste

3/4 cup vegetable oil, divided

1/2 pound andouille sausage, cut into 1/2-inch pieces

1/2 pound tasso, cut into 1/2-inch pieces

3/4 cup all-purpose flour

2 medium onions, chopped

6 green onions, chopped, white and green parts separated

1 green bell pepper, chopped

3 celery stalks, chopped

1 tablespoon minced garlic

6 1/2 cups chicken stock or water, or a combination of the two

3 bay leaves

Creole seasoning, to taste

3 tablespoons chopped flat-leaf parsley

Cooked long-grain white rice, for serving

Cut the hen into pieces as you would cut a chicken. Because the breast is large, cut it into 3 pieces. Use the back bone and any giblets, except the liver. Rinse, dry, and sprinkle liberally on all sides with salt and peppers.

Using a very large, heavy pot, heat 1/4 cup of the oil and brown the hen well on all sides. Remove the hen from the pot and set aside.

Add the remaining oil and the flour to the pot and stir constantly over high heat until the roux turns light brown. Reduce the heat to medium and cook, stirring constantly, until the roux is dark brown (the color of milk chocolate or a little darker).

Reduce the heat to low; add the onions, the white parts of the green onions, the bell pepper, the celery, and the garlic and sauté until translucent. Gradually stir in the stock and/or water. Add the bay leaves and season with Creole seasoning, cover, and simmer for 3 hours, stirring occasionally. As the gumbo cooks, skim the fat from the surface. You may skim as much as 1 cup of fat.

When the gumbo is cooked and the hen is tender, remove the bay leaves and stir in the green onion tops and parsley. Serve in bowls over the rice.

19. Quail Gumbo

MAKES 8 SERVINGS

INGREDIENTS

8 fresh quail or frozen, thawed

Salt and freshly ground black pepper, to taste

1 pound boudin or about 4 cups homemade jambalaya (or use a quick mix like Zatarain's or Oak Grove)

3/4 cup vegetable oil

3/4 cup all-purpose flour

1 large onion, chopped

3 green onions, chopped, white and green parts separated

1 green bell pepper, chopped

4 large garlic cloves, minced

1/4 pound tasso or andouille (or other smoked) sausage, cut into bite-size pieces

2 tablespoons tomato paste

6 cups homemade or canned chicken stock

1 teaspoon dried thyme

3 bay leaves

1/2 teaspoon Creole seasoning

1/2 teaspoon celery salt

3 tablespoons chopped flat-leaf parsley

Rinse the quail and remove any remaining feathers. Dry well and season with salt and pepper inside and out. If using boudin, remove it from the casings. Stuff each quail with about 4 tablespoons boudin or jambalaya and tie string around each quail from back to front, crossing the legs to hold in the stuffing.

In a wide, heavy pot, heat 3 tablespoons of the oil and carefully brown the quail lightly on all sides, moving them about to keep the skin from sticking. Remove the quail from the pot and set aside.

Add the remaining oil and the flour to the pot and stir constantly over medium-high heat until the roux begins to brown. Reduce the heat to medium and cook, stirring constantly, until the roux is the color of peanut butter.

Reduce the heat to low and add the onions and the white parts of the green onions, caramelizing them for about 5 minutes. Add the bell pepper and cook until wilted. Add the garlic and cook 1 more minute. Add the tomato paste and tasso and cook a few minutes more. Gradually stir in the stock, followed by all the seasonings except the green onion tops and parsley. Bring to a boil and then reduce the heat to medium-low.

Return the quail to the pot, cover, and simmer for 30 minutes. When done, add the green onion tops and remove the bay leaves.

To serve, place 1 quail in each bowl of gumbo and sprinkle with parsley.

20. Gumbo z'Herbes

MAKES 8 SERVINGS

INGREDIENTS

1 small ham bone or 1/2 pound smoked ham cubes

1 pint shucked oysters with their liquor

1/2 cup vegetable oil

1/2 cup all-purpose flour

1 large onion, chopped

3 green onions, chopped

3 celery stalks, chopped

3 garlic cloves, minced

1/2 teaspoon Creole seasoning

3 bay leaves

1/2 teaspoon dried thyme

1 tablespoon sugar

2 cups cleaned and roughly chopped mustard greens

2 cups cleaned and roughly chopped turnip greens

4 cups cleaned and roughly chopped collard greens

4 cups spinach

1 bunch flat-leaf parsley

1/2 small cabbage, chopped or shredded

2 cups endive, torn in pieces

Salt and freshly ground black pepper, to taste

Cooked long-grain white rice, for serving

If using a ham bone, simmer it in a large pot in 2 quarts of water, covered, for 2 hours or until the meat is about to fall off the bone. When cool enough to handle, remove the meat from the bone and set aside. Discard the bone and save the stock (you will need about 7 cups).

Strain the oysters, reserving their liquor, and check for shell fragments. You should have about 1/2 cup of liquor.

In a very large, heavy pot, combine the oil and flour and stir over high heat until the roux starts to brown. Reduce the heat to medium and cook, stirring constantly, until the roux becomes the color of milk chocolate. Immediately add the onions and simmer until caramelized. Add the celery and garlic and simmer a minute more.

Stir in the reserved ham stock, oyster liquor (about 1/2 cup), Creole seasoning, bay leaves, thyme, sugar, reserved ham or ham cubes, and greens and season with salt and pepper. Simmer, covered, for about 1 hour. Add the oysters and cook until they curl, about 1 minute. Taste and adjust the seasonings. Turn off the heat and remove the bay leaves.

Serve in Gumbo bowls over the rice.

21. Filé Gumbo

MAKES 6-8 SERVINGS

INGREDIENTS

2 pounds shrimp in shells with heads

1/2 cup vegetable oil or bacon drippings

1/2 cup all-purpose flour

1 onion, chopped

1 green bell pepper, chopped

3 garlic cloves, minced

2 tablespoons tomato paste

2 bay leaves

1/2 teaspoon salt, or to taste

1/2 teaspoon freshly ground black pepper, or to taste

1/2 teaspoon cayenne pepper, or to taste

2 tablespoons filé powder

1 pound jumbo lump crabmeat

Cooked long-grain white rice, for serving

De-head, peel, and devein the shrimp, placing the heads and shells in a medium pot. Add enough water to cover the shells by at least 2 inches and bring to a boil. Cover, reduce the heat, and simmer for 30 minutes. When slightly cooled, strain the stock into a large measuring cup and discard the shells. If necessary, add enough water to the stock to make 5 cups of liquid. Set aside.

In a large, heavy pot, combine the oil and flour. Stir constantly over high heat until the flour begins to brown. Reduce the heat to medium and stir constantly until the roux turns dark brown.

Add the onions and bell pepper and cook until wilted. Add the garlic and cook a minute more. Stir in the tomato paste and simmer for 5 minutes, stirring occasionally. Gradually stir in the shrimp stock. Add all the seasonings except the filé, cover, and simmer over low heat for 30 minutes.

Add the shrimp and continue cooking for 3 minutes if the shrimp are small or 7 minutes if large. Turn off the heat. If you are serving all of the gumbo immediately, add the filé and mix well. (If not, reserve the filé to add to individual bowls.) Gently stir in the crabmeat.

Serve in bowls over the hot rice. If you have not added the filé, add 1/2-3/4 teaspoon to each bowl, depending on the size of the bowls.

22. Catfish Gumbo

MAKES 6-8 SERVINGS

INGREDIENTS

3 pounds catfish nuggets, divided

1/2 cup canola or other vegetable oil

1/2 cup all-purpose flour

1 large onion, chopped, peels and trimmings reserved

1 green bell pepper, chopped, seeds and trimmings reserved

2 celery stalks, chopped

6 green onions, chopped, white and green parts separated

3 large garlic cloves, minced

1 (10-ounce) can original Ro-tel tomatoes with chilies

2 cups chopped fresh or canned diced tomatoes

3 cups stock

1/2 cup white wine

3 bay leaves

1/2 teaspoon dried thyme

1 teaspoon fresh lemon juice

1/2 teaspoon Worcestershire sauce

1 1/2 teaspoons Creole seasoning

Salt and freshly ground pepper, to taste

2 tablespoons chopped flat-leaf parsley

Cooked long-grain white rice, for serving

Cut 2 pounds of the catfish nuggets into 1-inch cubes and set aside. Place the remaining nuggets in a small pot with 4 cups of water and the trimmings from the vegetables to make stock. Cover and simmer for 45 minutes. Strain the stock into a large measuring cup and discard the solids.

Heat the oil in a large, heavy pot. Add the flour and stir constantly over medium heat to make a medium-dark roux the color of peanut butter. Add the onion, the white parts of the green onions, the bell pepper, and the celery and cook until wilted. Add the garlic and cook 1 minute more.

Add the tomatoes, 3 cups of the stock, the wine, bay leaves, thyme, lemon juice, Worcestershire sauce, and Creole seasoning and season with salt and pepper. Bring to a boil. Reduce the heat, cover, and simmer for 30 minutes, stirring occasionally.

Add the cubed catfish and bring to a boil. Reduce the heat and simmer until the fish is cooked through, about 5 minutes. Remove the bay leaves and add the parsley and green onion tops. Cover and let the gumbo rest for an hour or so.

Reheat the gumbo and serve in bowls over the rice.

23. Cabbage Gumbo

MAKES 4-6 SERVINGS

INGREDIENTS

1 large cabbage (about 3 pounds)

4 thick slices bacon

1/4 cup vegetable oil (more or less as needed)

1/2 cup all-purpose flour

1 onion, chopped

1 green bell pepper, chopped

2 celery stalks, chopped

3 large garlic cloves, minced

Salt and freshly ground black pepper, to taste

1 teaspoon sugar

3 bay leaves

1 teaspoon Creole seasoning

8 cups water

1 (10-ounce) can original Ro-tel tomatoes with green chilies

2 small smoked ham hocks

Cooked long-grain white rice, for serving

Cut the cabbage into bite-size pieces; rinse, drain, and set aside.

In a large, heavy pot, cook the bacon until crisp. Remove the bacon from the pot and reserve. Carefully pour the bacon grease into a large measuring cup and add enough oil to make 1/2 cup. Return the grease to the pan and add the flour; stir constantly over medium heat to make a light-brown or butterscotch-colored roux.

Add the onions, bell pepper, and celery and sauté until wilted. Add the garlic and sauté a minute more. Stir in the remaining ingredients and the cabbage and bring to a boil. Reduce the heat, cover, and simmer for 1 hour, stirring occasionally.

Serve in bowls over the rice and top with crumbled reserved bacon. Serve hot sauce on the side.

24. Turkey Gumbo

MAKES 6-8 SERVINGS

INGREDIENTS

1 or more turkey carcasses and leftover turkey

1/2 cup vegetable oil

1/2 cup all-purpose flour

1 onion, chopped

1 bunch green onions, chopped

3 celery stalks, chopped

3 garlic cloves, minced

Leftover turkey gravy (optional)

2 bay leaves

1/2 teaspoon dried thyme

Salt, Creole seasoning, and freshly ground black pepper, to taste

1/2 pound andouille (or other smoked) sausage, cut into bite-size pieces

1 pint shucked oysters (optional)

3 tablespoons chopped flat-leaf parsley

Cooked long-grain white rice, for serving

Remove any meat from the turkey carcass. Cut into chunks, along with leftover turkey. Set aside.

Place the turkey bones in a stock pot, cover with water, and bring to a boil. Reduce the heat to low, cover, and simmer for 1 hour. When cool enough to handle, strain the stock into a large measuring cup and discard the bones. If using oysters, strain the oyster liquor into the stock. If necessary, add water to make at least 8 cups of liquid. Set aside.

In a large, heavy pot, heat the oil over medium-high heat. Add the flour and stir constantly until the roux begins to brown. Reduce the heat to medium and cook, stirring constantly, until the roux becomes the color of peanut butter.

Add the onions and celery and simmer over low heat until translucent. Add the garlic and cook a minute more. Add 8 cups of the stock (or more if you prefer a thinner gumbo; if you have leftover turkey gravy, add it at this point).

Add all of the seasonings (except the parsley) and the sausage; cover and simmer for 30 minutes. Add the turkey meat and oysters, if using, and cook until the oysters curl, 1-2 minutes. Remove the bay leaves and adjust the seasonings. Add the parsley and serve in bowls over the rice.

25. Roux-less Gumbo

MAKES 6-8 SERVINGS

INGREDIENTS

2 pounds medium shrimp in shells with heads or 1 pound peeled and deveined frozen shrimp, thawed

3 cups sliced fresh okra or 3 cups frozen cut okra, thawed

1 pound boneless chicken thighs, cut into 1-inch pieces

Creole seasoning for sprinkling chicken plus 1/2 teaspoon

1 teaspoon plus 3 tablespoons vegetable oil

1 large onion, chopped

1 green bell pepper, chopped

1 bunch green onions, chopped, green and white parts separated

2 celery stalks, chopped

3 garlic cloves, minced

1 (15-ounce) can crushed tomatoes

4 cups shrimp and/or chicken stock

1/2 teaspoon salt

10 grinds on a black pepper mill

1 teaspoon celery salt

1 heaping tablespoon chopped flat-leaf parsley

1 tablespoon filé powder

Cooked long-grain white rice, for serving

If using fresh shrimp, remove the heads and shells and devein the shrimp. Place the shells and heads in a medium pot, add enough water to cover the shells by at least 2 inches, and bring to a boil. Cover, reduce the heat to low, and simmer for 30 minutes. When slightly cooled, strain the stock into a large measuring cup and discard the shells. You'll need 4 cups of stock. Reserve the rest for a later use.

Heat 1 teaspoon of the oil in a skillet over medium heat and add the okra. Cook, turning often, until all the sliminess is removed from okra. Set aside.

Sprinkle the chicken on all sides with Creole seasoning. Heat the remaining oil in large, heavy pot and, in 2 batches, brown the chicken pieces on all sides. Remove the chicken to a plate.

Add the onion, the white parts of the green onions, the bell pepper, and the celery to the pot and sauté until translucent. Add the garlic and sauté a minute more.

Return the chicken to the pot and add the okra, tomatoes, stock, remaining Creole seasoning, salt, pepper, and celery salt. Cover and simmer for 30 minutes.

Add the shrimp, green onion tops, and parsley and cook 5-10 minutes longer, or until the shrimp are just pink. Add the filé to the pot if you intend to serve all the gumbo. Serve in bowls over the rice. If you have not added the filé, add 1/2-3/4 teaspoon to each bowl.

26. Duck and Andouille Gumbo

MAKES 6-8 SERVINGS

INGREDIENTS

1 (6-pound) duckling

2 onions, 1 quartered and the other chopped

4 celery stalks, 2 cut in chunks and the other 2 chopped

4 bay leaves, divided

Freshly ground black pepper, to taste

1 pound andouille sausage, cut into bite-size pieces

3/4 cup vegetable oil

1 cup all-purpose flour

1 bunch green onions, chopped, white and green parts separated

1 green bell pepper, chopped

4 garlic cloves, minced

1/2 teaspoon dried thyme

1/2 teaspoon Creole seasoning

1/4 teaspoon cayenne pepper

1 tablespoon Worcestershire sauce

Salt, to taste

1/2 cup chopped flat-leaf parsley

Cooked long-grain white rice, for serving

Rinse the duck and remove any excess fat. Place the duck in a large pot and cover with water. Add the quartered onion, celery chunks, 2 of the bay leaves, and several grinds on a pepper mill. Bring to a boil. Reduce the heat to low and simmer until the duck has cooked through, about 45 minutes. Remove the duck from that pot and let rest until cool enough to handle. Debone the duck and cut the meat into bite-size pieces. Set the meat aside.

Return the bones to the pot and simmer for 1 hour. Strain the stock into a large bowl and let cool. Refrigerate until the fat hardens and skim and discard the fat.

In a large skillet, brown the sausage over medium-high heat. Set aside.

Heat the oil in a large, heavy pot over high heat; add the flour and stir constantly until the roux begins to brown. Reduce the heat to medium or medium-low and cook, stirring constantly, until the roux is the color of dark chocolate.

Add the chopped onion, the white parts of the green onions, the celery, and the bell pepper and cook, stirring, until wilted. Add the garlic and cook a minute more. Gradually stir in 6 cups of the stock. (If you have extra stock, freeze it for another use.)

Add the remaining bay leaves and the thyme, Creole seasoning, cayenne pepper, and Worcestershire sauce and season with salt.

Add the sausage and duck and simmer, covered, until the duck is tender, about 1 hour. Stir in the parsley and green onion tops.

Serve in bowls over the rice with hot sauce and hot French bread on the side.

27. Braised Goose and Foie Gras Jambalaya

MAKES 4-6 SERVINGS

INGREDIENTS

1 cup goose meat

6 ounces foie gras, chopped

12 garlic cloves, peeled and minced

1 onion, medium diced

2 green bell peppers, medium diced

6 celery stalks, medium diced

2 bay leaves

1 teaspoon cayenne pepper

4 tablespoons kosher salt, or to taste

1/2 cup red wine

2 cups rice

4 cups poultry stock

1 tablespoon chopped fresh sage

1 tablespoon chopped fresh thyme

Cook the goose meat in a medium skillet over high heat, stirring, until it has browned. Reduce the heat to low, add a small amount of water, cover tightly, and cook until the meat is tender, about 1-2 hours.

Place a heavy-bottom braising pan over medium-high heat. Add the foie gras to the pan and swirl to melt for 5 seconds. Add the garlic, onion, bell pepper, celery, bay leaves, cayenne, and salt. Swirl evenly with a wooden spoon for 3-5 minutes or until the onion is translucent and the vegetables are soft and starting to brown.

Add the wine and stir constantly to deglaze the pan, allowing the liquid to completely evaporate.

Add the meat, rice, and stock, and bring the jambalaya to a simmer. Reduce the heat, cover the pan, and cook for 10 minutes. Turn off the heat, keep the pan covered, and continue to steam until the rice is cooked all the way. Fluff the rice with a fork, and add the sage and thyme.

28. Black Jambalaya

MAKES 10-12 SERVINGS

INGREDIENTS

1/4 cup vegetable oil

1 pound Louisiana smoked sausage, such as andouille, chaurice, or green onion, cut into 1/4-inch-thick rounds

1 large onion, diced

3 celery stalks, diced

2 poblano peppers, diced

1/4 cup minced garlic

1/2 pound smoked pork butt (see Note)

1/2 pound smoked chicken thighs (see Note)

1 (12-ounce) can black-eyed peas

4 cups stock, preferably pork (see Note)

2 tablespoons chopped fresh oregano

2 tablespoons chopped flat-leaf parsley

2 tablespoons chopped fresh thyme

1 tablespoon kosher salt

1 teaspoon freshly ground black pepper

1 teaspoon cayenne pepper

2 cups Uncle Ben's long-grain rice

In a large, heavy pot, preferably black cast) iron, heat the oil over medium heat. Add the sausage and cook until it curls. Add the onions, celery, peppers, and garlic and sauté until translucent. Add the pork and cook 5 minutes, stirring frequently. Add the chicken and cook another 5 minutes. Add the black-eyed peas and cook another 5 minutes.

Add stock and bring to a simmer. Add the herbs and seasonings and then the rice and bring to a simmer. Cover and cook over low heat until the rice is done, about 30 minutes.

NOTE * If you don't want to smoke the pork or chicken, you can braise it. To braise the pork, rub it with salt and pepper and brown it on all sides in a black iron skillet, then cook it in water on the stovetop or in the oven until the meat falls off the bone. You can then use the braising liquid for the stock. To prepare the chicken, rub it with salt and pepper and brown it on all sides over high temperature until it caramelizes and is 75 percent cooked before adding it in bite-size chunks to the jambalaya.

29. Chicken, Shrimp, and Sausage Jambalaya

MAKES 6-8 SERVINGS

INGREDIENTS

1 chicken, cut into 10 pieces, splitting the breast into fourths
Salt, freshly ground black pepper, and Creole seasoning, to taste

1/4 cup vegetable oil

1 pound smoked sausage, preferably pork, cut into 1/4-inch-thick rounds

1 large onion, chopped

6 green onions, chopped, green and white parts separated

1 green bell pepper, chopped

2 celery stalks, chopped

4 garlic cloves, minced

3 cups water, or more as needed

1/2 teaspoon salt

1/2 teaspoon freshly ground black pepper

1 tablespoon Creole seasoning

1 1/2 cups long-grain white rice

2 pounds shrimp, peeled and deveined, or 1 pound medium peeled and deveined frozen shrimp, thawed

1/3 cup minced Italian flat-leaf parsley

Rinse the chicken pieces and pat dry. Season on all sides with salt, freshly ground black pepper, and Creole seasoning. Heat the oil in a large, heavy pot. When hot, brown the chicken on all sides and remove to paper towels. Brown the sausage and remove from pot.

If necessary, add enough extra oil to cover the bottom of pot. Add the onion, the white parts of the green onions, the bell pepper, and the celery and sauté until transparent. Add the garlic and sauté a minute more. Add the water and seasonings and bring to a boil over high heat. Add the rice, cover, and reduce the heat to low. Simmer for 20 minutes. Gently stir in the shrimp (at this point, there still should be some liquid at the bottom of the pot. If not, add 1/4 cup water for moisture while the shrimp cook), the green onion tops, and the parsley and simmer 10 more minutes, or until the water has been absorbed. Stir gently so as not to break up the Ingredients.

Serve hot with hot French bread and salad and Louisiana hot sauce on the side.

30. Crawfish and Sausage Jambalaya

MAKES 8-10 SERVINGS

INGREDIENTS

3 tablespoons vegetable oil

1 medium onion, chopped

1 bunch green onions, chopped, white and green parts separated

1 green bell pepper, chopped

2 celery stalks, chopped

3 garlic cloves, minced

1 pound smoked sausage, cut into 1/4-inch-thick rounds

1 (14.5-ounce) can diced tomatoes

1 tablespoon tomato paste

3 cups seafood stock, preferably, or chicken stock or water

1/2 teaspoon dried thyme

1/4 teaspoon Creole seasoning

1/2 teaspoon salt

1/2 teaspoon freshly ground black pepper

1 teaspoon Worcestershire sauce

1 1/2 cups rice

1 pound Louisiana crawfish tails with fat

2 tablespoons chopped flat-leaf parsley

Heat the oil in a large, heavy pot. Add the onion, the white parts of the green onions, the bell pepper, and the celery and sauté until transparent. Add the garlic and sausage and sauté a couple of minutes more. Add the tomatoes, tomato paste, and stock and bring to a boil. Add the seasonings except the parsley, reduce the heat to low, cover, and simmer for 5 minutes. Return to a boil and add the rice. Reduce the heat again and simmer, covered, for 10 minutes. Add the crawfish and green onion tops and simmer until the liquid has been absorbed, about 20 more minutes. Remove from the heat and top with the parsley.

31. Pastalaya

MAKES 6-8 SERVINGS

INGREDIENTS

3 tablespoons vegetable oil such as canola

1/2 pound smoked sausage, cut into 1/2-inch-thick rounds

2 boneless, skinless chicken breasts, cut into bite-size cubes

1 large onion, chopped

1/2 green bell pepper, chopped

2 celery stalks, chopped

6 green onions, chopped

3 large garlic cloves, minced

1 (14.5-ounce) can diced tomatoes

3 cups chicken broth, homemade or canned

1/2 teaspoon dried thyme

1/2 teaspoon Creole seasoning

Salt and freshly ground black pepper, to taste

12 ounces spaghetti or other pasta

Heat the oil to hot in a large, heavy pot. Brown the sausage on both sides over high heat and remove from the pot. Brown the chicken cubes and remove from pot. Reduce the heat to medium heat sauté the onion, bell pepper, celery, and green onions until wilted. Add the garlic and sauté a minute more. Add the tomatoes and chicken broth and return the sausage and chicken to the pot. Simmer, covered, for 15 minutes.

Add the pasta and stir it into the liquid. Simmer, covered, over medium-low heat, stirring occasionally, for 15 more minutes, or until the pasta is al dente and has absorbed most of the liquid.

32. Slow Cooker Jambalaya

MAKES 6-8 SERVINGS

INGREDIENTS

1 1/2 pounds boneless chicken thighs, rinsed, trimmed of excess fat, and cut into 1-inch cubes

3 links Cajun smoked sausage (about 14 ounces total), cut into 1/4-inch-thick rounds

1 medium onion, chopped

1 green bell pepper, chopped

1 celery stalk, chopped

3 garlic cloves, minced

2 tablespoons tomato paste

1 teaspoon Creole seasoning

1 teaspoon salt

1/2 teaspoon freshly ground black pepper

1/2 teaspoon Tabasco sauce

1/2 teaspoon Worcestershire sauce

2 cups chicken broth

1 1/2 cups long-grain rice

2 pounds medium shrimp, peeled and deveined (optional)

Place all the Ingredients (except the shrimp, if using) into a slow cooker. Stir together, cover, and cook on low for 5 hours.

If using shrimp, gently stir them in after the 5 hours of cooking and cook on high for 30 minutes to 1 hour more, or until the shrimp are done but not overcooked.

LAGNIAPPE

33. Crawfish Bisque

MAKES 4 SERVINGS

INGREDIENTS

3 tablespoons plus 1/2 cup vegetable oil, divided

2 pounds fresh crawfish tails, divided, or 2 frozen (1-pound) packages, thawed, divided

1 onion, chopped and divided

1 bunch green onions, chopped and divided

1 green bell pepper, chopped and divided

3 garlic cloves, minced and divided

3/4 teaspoon salt, divided

3/4 teaspoon freshly ground black pepper, divided

3/4 teaspoon Creole seasoning, divided

2 cups bread crumbs, made in a food processor from stale French bread

1 egg, beaten

2/3 cup plus 1/2 cup all-purpose flour, divided

5 cups seafood stock or water

2 tablespoons tomato paste

Pinch cayenne pepper, or to taste

2 cups cooked long-grain white rice

2 tablespoons chopped flat-leaf parsley

Heat the oven to 350°. Spray a large baking sheet with nonstick cooking spray and set aside.

Heat 3 tablespoons of the oil in a large skillet and sauté half the onions, green onions, bell pepper, and garlic. Add 1 pound of the crawfish and sauté for 5 minutes. Remove the mixture to a food processor and grind to the consistency of ground meat. Transfer the mixture to a bowl and add 1/4 teaspoon of the salt, 1/4 teaspoon of the pepper, 1/4 teaspoon of the Creole seasoning, the bread crumbs, and the egg and combine well.

Place 2/3 cup of the flour in a shallow baking dish. Roll the mixture into 1-inch balls. Roll the balls in the flour and place them on the baking sheet. Bake, turning the balls several times, until lightly browned all over, about 35 minutes. Set aside.

Heat the remaining oil in a medium, heavy pot over medium-high heat. Add the remaining flour, stirring constantly, until it turns a peanut butter color. Add the remaining onions, bell pepper, and garlic, and cook until translucent. Add the stock or water, tomato paste, the remaining salt, pepper, and Creole seasoning, and the cayenne pepper, and simmer, covered, for 15 minutes.

Mince the remaining crawfish tails and add to the bisque and continue cooking for 15 minutes. For a smooth bisque, blend with a hand blender. Add the crawfish balls and simmer for 5 more minutes.

Serve in bowls over the rice. Sprinkle with parsley.

34. Crawfish Étouffée

MAKES 8-10 SERVINGS OR ENOUGH FOR A CROWD AT A PARTY BUFFET

INGREDIENTS

3/4 cup butter or vegetable oil

3/4 cup all-purpose flour

1 large onion, chopped

1 bunch green onions, chopped, white and green parts separated

1 green bell pepper, chopped

3 celery stalks, chopped.

4 large garlic cloves, minced

3 tablespoons tomato paste

6 cups seafood stock or water (see Note)

1/2 teaspoon dried thyme

3 bay leaves

1 teaspoon Creole seasoning

1 teaspoon salt

1 tablespoon fresh lemon juice

Cayenne pepper and freshly ground black pepper, to taste

2-3 pounds crawfish tails with fat

3 tablespoons chopped flat-leaf parsley

Cooked long-grain white rice, for serving

In a large, heavy pot, melt the butter or heat the oil over medium heat. Add the flour and stir constantly. If using butter, cook the roux until it turns a blonde or golden color. If using oil, continue cooking, stirring, until the roux is medium brown. Add the onions, the white parts of the green onions, the bell peppers, the celery, and the garlic and sauté, stirring, until translucent.

Add the tomato paste, stock or water, thyme, bay leaves, Creole seasoning, salt, and lemon juice, season with the cayenne and pepper, and bring to a boil. Reduce the heat, cover, and simmer for 20 minutes, stirring occasionally and skimming any fat off the top. Add the crawfish, parsley, and green onion tops, bring to a boil, reduce the heat, and simmer for 10 minutes. Remove the bay leaves.

When ready to serve, reheat gently and serve over the rice.

35. Crawfish Pies

MAKES 5 (5-INCH) INDIVIDUAL PIES

INGREDIENTS

Enough dough for four 9-inch pies (store-bought is fine)

2 pounds crawfish tails with fat, divided

6 tablespoons butter

6 tablespoons all-purpose flour

2 medium onions, chopped

1 green bell pepper, chopped

4 garlic cloves, minced

2 cups half-and-half

4 tablespoons sherry

2 tablespoons fresh lemon juice

1 teaspoon salt

15 turns on a black pepper mill

1 teaspoon cayenne pepper

4 tablespoons chopped flat-leaf parsley

1 egg white, beaten

Preheat the oven to 350°.

Roll out the pie dough to 1/8-inch thickness. You should have enough dough for five 5-inch double-crusted pies. To get the right size for the bottom crusts, place one of the pans upside-down on the dough and cut the dough 1 inch from the edge of the pan. The top crusts should be cut at 5 inches for the best fit. Place the bottom crusts into the pie pans and keep the top crusts cold in the refrigerator.

In a food processor, chop half the crawfish tails until nearly ground. Leave the others whole.

Melt the butter in a medium, heavy pot or large skillet over medium heat. Add the flour and stir constantly until the roux is light brown. Add the onion and bell pepper and sauté for about 5 minutes. Add the garlic and sauté 1 minute more. Add the half-and-half, sherry, lemon juice, salt, pepper, cayenne, and parsley and cook for 5 minutes. Add the chopped and whole crawfish and cook 5 minutes more.

Fill each of the prepared pie shells with about 1 cup of the crawfish filling. Cover with the top crusts and crimp the edges. Cut several slits in the top crust and brush with the egg white. Place the pies on cookie sheets and bake until the filling is bubbly and the crusts are golden brown, about 1 hour.

36. Dirty Rice

MAKES 8-10 SERVINGS

INGREDIENTS

3 cups water

1 1/2 cups long-grain white rice

1/4 plus 1 teaspoon salt, divided

2 tablespoons vegetable oil

1 onion, chopped

6 green onions, chopped, white and green parts separated

1 green bell pepper, chopped

2 celery stalks, chopped

3 garlic cloves, minced

1 pound ground beef

1 pound chicken livers, chopped

1/2 teaspoon freshly ground black pepper

1/2 teaspoon cayenne pepper

1/3 cup chopped flat-leaf parsley

Bring the water to boil in a medium saucepan. Add the rice and 1/4 teaspoon of the salt. Reduce the heat to low, cover, and cook until all the water has been absorbed, about 20 minutes.

In a medium, heavy pot, heat the oil and sauté the onion, the white parts of the green onions, the bell pepper, and the celery until translucent. Add the garlic and sauté a minute more. Add the ground beef and brown, stirring. Add the chicken livers and continue cooking and stirring until the beef and livers are cooked through, about 10 minutes. Add the pepper and cayenne, cover, and simmer for 5 minutes.

Stir in the parsley and green onion tops. Gently fold in the rice. Serve with Louisiana hot sauce on the side.

37. Eggs Sardou

MAKES 4 SERVINGS

INGREDIENTS

FOR THE HOLLANDAISE SAUCE

2 large egg yolks

1 1/2 tablespoons fresh lemon juice

2 sticks unsalted butter

Salt and freshly ground black pepper, to taste

FOR THE EGGS

2 (9-ounce) bags fresh spinach

1 tablespoon olive oil

1 teaspoon minced garlic

1/3 cup heavy cream

Salt and freshly ground black pepper, to taste

8 fresh-cooked or canned artichoke bottoms

2 tablespoons white vinegar

8 eggs

To make the sauce, place the egg yolks and lemon juice in a blender. Pulse several times to mix.

Melt the butter in a glass pitcher in the microwave, being careful not to boil it. Gradually pour the butter into the egg mixture and blend until a thickened, creamy sauce forms. Season with salt and pepper.

To make the eggs, prepare the spinach by sautéing it in the olive oil in a saucepan, stirring, just until wilted and still bright green. Stir in the cream, season with salt and pepper, and keep warm.

Heat the artichoke bottoms and keep warm.

Fill a skillet or shallow pot with 2 1/2 inches of water. Add the vinegar and heat to medium hot.

One at a time, crack 4 of the eggs into a small cup and gently pour them into the water. Simmer the eggs until they rise to the top of the liquid, and then turn them over with a spoon. Cook until the whites are set but the yolks are still runny. Remove with a slotted spoon and pat dry with paper towels. Repeat with the remaining eggs.

Spoon a serving of the spinach on each of 4 plates. Place 2 artichoke bottoms on each plate on top of the spinach and place an egg on each artichoke. Spoon the hollandaise sauce over all and serve immediately.

38. Grits and Grillades

MAKES 6 SERVINGS

INGREDIENTS

1 (3-pound) beef or veal round steak, pounded to about 1/4 inch thick

Salt and freshly ground black pepper, to taste

1 cup all-purpose flour

3/4 cup vegetable oil, divided

1 large onion, chopped

1 green bell pepper, chopped

1 bunch green onions, chopped, green and white parts separated

3 garlic cloves, minced

1 large tomato, chopped

1 tablespoon tomato paste

1/2 cup red wine

3 cups water

1 teaspoon red wine vinegar

1/2 teaspoon dried thyme

1 tablespoon Worcestershire sauce

Salt, freshly ground black pepper, and Creole seasoning, to taste

3 tablespoons chopped flat-leaf parsley

Grits to serve 6, cooked according to package **DIRECTIONS**

Cut the beef into roughly 2 × 3-inch pieces. Season both sides liberally with salt and pepper.

Heat 1/4 cup of the oil in a large, heavy skillet and place the flour in a shallow bowl or plate. Dredge each piece of steak in the flour, shake off the excess, and brown on both sides. Transfer the meat to paper towels.

Add the remaining oil to the skillet and sauté the onions, the white parts of the green onions, the bell pepper, and the garlic until translucent. Add the tomato, tomato paste, wine, water, vinegar, thyme, Worcestershire sauce, and meat and season with salt, pepper, and Creole seasoning. Bring to a boil. Reduce the heat, cover, and simmer until the meat is tender, about 1 1/2 hours. Add the parsley and green onion tops and serve over the grits.

39. Natchitoches Meat Pies

MAKES ABOUT 24

INGREDIENTS

2 tablespoons vegetable oil

1 large onion, chopped

6 green onions, chopped

1 green bell pepper, chopped

3 garlic cloves, minced

1 pound ground beef

1 pound ground pork

1 teaspoon Creole seasoning

1/2 teaspoon salt

1/2 teaspoon freshly ground black pepper

1/4 teaspoon cayenne pepper

1/4 cup all-purpose flour

1 package (2 crusts) refrigerated piecrusts

2 egg whites, beaten

In a large, heavy skillet, heat the oil. Add vegetables and sauté until translucent. Add the meat and cook, stirring occasionally, over high heat for a few minutes. Reduce the heat and continue to cook, chopping up the meat with a spoon, until it is thoroughly browned. Add the seasonings and flour and continue to cook for 10 minutes. Remove from the heat. The filling can be made ahead and refrigerated until you are ready to use it.

When you are ready to make the pies, preheat the oven to 350°. Spray 2 cookie sheets with nonstick cooking spray.

Place the refrigerated piecrusts on a flat surface and roll them out slightly thinner. Using a medium biscuit cutter, cut out circles. Place a heaping tablespoon of the filling on one half of each circle, leaving the edge clear. This will be the bottom of the pie. Fill a small bowl with water. Dip a finger in the water and wet the edge of the bottom half of the dough and fold the top over to form a turnover. Seal the edges together with the tines of a fork and place the pies about 1 inch apart on the prepared cookie sheets.

Brush the pies with egg whites and make a couple of small slits in the top of each pie. Bake until golden brown.

40. Oyster Artichoke Gumbo

MAKES 6-8 SERVINGS

INGREDIENTS

3 dozen shucked oysters with their liquor, plus extra liquor, if available

1 stick butter

1/2 cup all-purpose flour

1 large onion, chopped

6 green onions, chopped, white and green parts separated

2 celery stalks, chopped

4 large garlic cloves, minced

6 cups oyster liquor and seafood stock (or, in a pinch, chicken stock)

1 (14-ounce) can quartered artichoke hearts, drained and cut into bite-size pieces

1/4 teaspoon cayenne pepper

1 teaspoon Creole seasoning

1/2 teaspoon celery salt

1 teaspoon Worcestershire sauce

Salt and freshly ground black pepper, to taste

1 cup half-and-half

2 tablespoons chopped flat-leaf parsley

Strain the oysters and reserve the liquor. Check the oysters for shell fragments and set aside.

In a heavy pot, melt the butter over low heat and add the flour, stirring constantly, until thick and just beginning to turn brown (a blonde roux). Add the onion, the white parts of the green onions, and the celery and sauté until wilted. Add the garlic and sauté another minute.

Add the oyster liquor, stock, artichokes, cayenne pepper, Creole seasoning, celery salt, and Worcestershire sauce and season with salt and pepper (start with just a small amount of salt since the oysters may be salty). Cover and simmer for 10 minutes. Add the half-and-half, bring almost to a boil, and add the oysters. Reduce the heat and simmer for several minutes or until the oysters curl. Turn off the heat and stir in the green onion tops and parsley. Adjust the seasonings before serving.

41. Oyster Dressing

MAKES 8-10 SERVINGS

INGREDIENTS

1 day-old loaf French bread, torn into bite-size pieces

3 dozen shucked oysters, strained and liquor reserved

Oyster liquor plus enough chicken or turkey stock to make 2 cups

1 stick butter

1 onion, chopped

1 bunch green onions, chopped

3 celery stalks, chopped

3 garlic cloves, minced

3 tablespoons chopped flat-leaf parsley

1/2 teaspoon salt, or to taste

12 turns on a black pepper mill

1/2 teaspoon cayenne pepper, or to taste

1 teaspoon ground sage

2 eggs, beaten

Place the bread in a large bowl, cover with the stock, and let soak for 1 hour. Check the oysters and remove any shell fragments.

Preheat the oven to 350°. Melt the butter in a skillet and sauté the onions and celery until translucent. Add the garlic and sauté a minute more. Add the vegetables to the bread, along with the parsley, seasonings, and eggs. Mix well.

Spread the dressing in an 11 × 13-inch baking dish or 2 smaller ones and bake until puffy and golden brown on top, about 45 minutes.

42. Oyster Pot Pie

MAKES 6 SERVINGS

INGREDIENTS

2 dozen large or 3 dozen small shucked oysters, with their liquor

1 cup sliced fresh mushrooms

1 tablespoon butter

4 tablespoons vegetable oil

4 tablespoons all-purpose flour

6 green onions, chopped, white and green parts separated

1/2 green bell pepper, chopped

1 celery stalk, chopped

2 large garlic cloves, minced

1/4 cup andouille sausage or smoked ham, chopped into 1/4-inch pieces

1 teaspoon Creole seasoning

1 teaspoon Worcestershire sauce

2 dashes of Tabasco sauce

2 tablespoons chopped flat-leaf parsley

Salt and freshly ground black pepper, to taste

2 piecrusts, homemade or store-bought, refrigerated

1 egg white, beaten

Strain the oysters, and pour the liquor into a large measuring cup; add enough water to make 1 cup. Check the oysters for shell fragments and set aside.

Heat the butter in a small skillet and sauté the mushrooms until they are limp. Set aside.

In a large skillet or medium pot, heat the oil over high heat; add the flour and stir constantly until the roux starts to brown. Reduce the heat to medium and cook, stirring constantly, until the roux is the color of milk chocolate. Add the onions, the white parts of the green onions, the bell pepper, and the celery and cook until wilted. Add the garlic and cook a minute more. Add the oyster liquor, sausage or ham, Creole seasoning, Worcestershire sauce, and Tabasco sauce. Cover, reduce the heat to a simmer, and cook for 15 minutes.

Turn up the heat to medium-high and add the mushrooms and oysters. Cook until the oysters curl, about 4 minutes. Turn off the heat and stir in the green onion tops and parsley. Season with salt and pepper. Cool.

Heat the oven to 350°. Place one of the crusts in the pie plate. Add the oyster mixture and cover with the top crust, crimping the edges. Cut several slits in the top crust to release steam, and brush the crust with the egg white. Bake for 45 minutes or until the pastry is browned.

43. Oyster Rockefeller Gumbo

MAKES 6 SERVINGS

INGREDIENTS

1 quart shucked oysters with their liquor, or 3 dozen oysters with 3-5 cups liquor

1 stick butter

1/2 cup all-purpose flour

1 bunch green onions, chopped

1/2 cup chopped green bell pepper

1/2 cup chopped celery

1 teaspoon minced garlic

1 (10-ounce) box frozen chopped spinach, thawed

1/4 cup chopped fresh sweet basil

5 cups oyster liquor and/or seafood stock

2 tablespoons Herbsaint or Pernod

1/2 teaspoon Creole seasoning

Tabasco sauce, to taste

2 teaspoons Worcestershire sauce

White pepper, to taste

1/2 cup chopped flat-leaf parsley

1 cup half-and-half

Salt, to taste

Strain the oysters, reserving the liquor. Check the oysters and discard any shell. Set aside.

Melt the butter in a large, heavy pot. Add the flour and stir constantly over medium heat to make a blonde roux. Add the onions, bell pepper, and celery and sauté until translucent. Add the garlic, spinach, and basil and sauté a minute more. Add the oyster liquor and/or seafood stock gradually and stir until well-blended. Add the Herbsaint or Pernod, Creole seasoning, Tabasco sauce, and Worcestershire sauce and season with pepper. Cover, reduce the heat to low, and simmer for 15 minutes.

Taste and adjust the seasonings. Add salt at this point, if needed, depending on how salty the oysters are. Add the parsley, half-and-half, and oysters and simmer until the oysters curl, a minute or 2. Serve with plenty of hot French bread.

44. Redfish Court Bouillon

MAKES 4-6 SERVINGS

INGREDIENTS

1 (3- to 4-pound) firm, white-fleshed fish such as redfish or red snapper

3 tablespoons extra-virgin olive oil

1 medium onion, chopped

3 green onions, chopped

1/2 green bell pepper, chopped

1 celery stalk, chopped

3 garlic cloves, minced

1 large tomato, chopped

1 (15-ounce) can tomato sauce

Juice of 1 lemon

1 tablespoon Worcestershire sauce

1/4 cup red wine

1/2 teaspoon dried thyme, or 2 teaspoons chopped fresh

1/2 teaspoon dried basil, or 2 teaspoons chopped fresh

1/2 teaspoon cayenne pepper

1 teaspoon sugar

Salt and freshly ground black pepper, to taste

2 tablespoons chopped flat-leaf parsley

Heat the oven to 350°. Remove any scales remaining on the fish and rinse well. Dry and place in a large baking dish with 2-inch sides. Refrigerate until the sauce is ready.

Heat the oil in a medium, heavy pot and sauté the onions, bell pepper, celery, and garlic until translucent. Add the tomatoes, tomato sauce, lemon juice, Worcestershire sauce, wine, thyme, basil, cayenne pepper, and sugar and season with salt and pepper. Bring to a boil, reduce the heat to low, and simmer, covered, for 30 minutes.

Add the parsley, taste, and adjust the seasonings.

Spread some of the sauce on the bottom of the baking pan. Sprinkle the fish with salt and pepper all over and place in the pan. Cover the fish with the sauce, placing some inside the body cavity. Bake, uncovered, for 30 minutes, or until the fish is just done at the center (using a knife, the flesh at the thickest part of the fish will easily pull away from the bone). Cover with foil and keep warm until serving.

45. Red Beans and Rice

MAKES 8-10 SERVINGS

INGREDIENTS

1 pound dried kidney beans

2 tablespoons vegetable oil

1 large onion, chopped

1 bunch green onions, chopped, white and green parts separated

1 green bell pepper, chopped

2 celery stalks, chopped

4 garlic cloves, minced

6 cups water

3 bay leaves

1/2 teaspoon dried thyme

1 teaspoon Creole seasoning

1 ham bone with some ham on it, preferably, or 2 ham hocks or 1/2 pound ham chunks

Salt and freshly ground black pepper, to taste

1 pound smoked sausage, cut into 1/2-inch-thick rounds

2 tablespoons chopped flat-leaf parsley, plus more for serving

Cooked long-grain white rice, for serving

Place the beans in a large pot, cover with water, soak overnight, and drain.

In a large, heavy pot, heat the oil and sauté the onions, the white parts of the green onions, the bell pepper, the celery and the garlic.

In a large skillet, brown the sausage. Set aside.

To the pot add the beans, water, bay leaves, thyme, Creole seasoning, and ham and bring to a boil. Reduce the heat, cover, and simmer for 2 hours, stirring occasionally, adding the sausage 30 minutes before the cooking is complete.

Remove the bay leaves, stir in the parsley, and serve in bowls with the rice. Sprinkle bowls with more parsley, if desired.

46. Shrimp and Grits

MAKES 6 SERVINGS

INGREDIENTS

3 pounds large shrimp (about 15 to 20 to the pound), peeled and deveined

5 tablespoons butter, divided

8 green onions, chopped

5 large garlic cloves, minced

Zest and juice of 1 lemon

1/3 cup dry white wine

1 tablespoon Worcestershire sauce

1 teaspoon Italian seasoning

Freshly ground black pepper, to taste

1/2 teaspoon plus 1/4 teaspoon salt, divided

1 teaspoon Creole seasoning

2 tablespoons chopped flat-leaf parsley

1 cup quick grits

4 1/4 cups water

1/4 cup freshly grated Parmesan

Melt 4 tablespoons of the butter in a large, heavy skillet over medium heat. Add the onions and garlic and sauté until wilted. Add the shrimp and sauté, stirring, for a few minutes until they turn pink. Add the lemon zest and juice, wine, Worcestershire sauce, Italian seasoning, pepper, Creole seasoning, and 1/2 teaspoon of the salt and simmer for about 3 minutes. Do not overcook the shrimp. Remove from the heat and sprinkle with parsley.

To cook the grits, bring the water to a boil in a large saucepan and add the grits in a steady stream while stirring. Add the remaining salt. Cover, reduce the heat to low, and simmer for about 10 minutes. Remove from the heat and stir in the Parmesan and remaining butter. Serve the shrimp over the grits on plates or in bowls.

47. Shrimp Rémoulade

MAKES 6-8 SERVINGS

INGREDIENTS

1/2 cup chopped green onions

1/2 cup chopped celery

1/4 cup chopped flat-leaf parsley

2 garlic cloves, minced

1/2 cup fresh horseradish (found in refrigerated section of grocery stores)

1/2 cup ketchup

3/4 cup Creole mustard

2 tablespoons Worcestershire sauce

3 tablespoons fresh lemon juice

1/8 teaspoon cayenne pepper

Salt, freshly ground black pepper, and cayenne pepper, to taste

3 pounds large peeled and deveined shrimp

Shredded lettuce, about 4 cups

In a bowl, combine all the Ingredients except the shrimp and lettuce and mix well. Taste and adjust the seasonings.

Several hours before serving, place the shrimp in a large bowl. Gradually stir in the sauce until the consistency is to your liking. Some may prefer all of the dressing and others, less. Serve over shredded lettuce.

48. Pepper Jelly

MAKES 8-10 SMALL JARS

INGREDIENTS

6-8 large jalapeño peppers, minced, to yield 1/2 cup

1/3 cup minced green bell peppers

6 1/2 cups sugar

1 1/2 cups red wine vinegar

1 (6-ounce) bottle Certo or 2 (3-ounce) packages

6 drops red or green food coloring

Remove the stems and seeds from the peppers and chop very fine or process in a food processor. Combine all the Ingredients except the Certo in a medium saucepan and mix well. Bring to a boil, and boil for 2-3 minutes, stirring often. Remove from the heat and stir in the Certo. Pour in sterilized jelly jars and seal.

Serve over cream cheese for spreading on crackers.

49. Stuffed Mirlitons

MAKES 6-8 SERVINGS (1-2 MIRLITON HALVES PER SERVING)

INGREDIENTS

6 mirlitons

7 tablespoons butter, divided

1 medium onion, chopped

1 bunch (6-8) green onions, chopped, white and green parts separated

2 celery stalks, chopped

4 garlic cloves, minced

1 teaspoon Italian seasoning

1 teaspoon Tabasco sauce

1 tablespoon fresh lemon juice

Salt and freshly ground black pepper, to taste

2 pounds medium shrimp, peeled and deveined, or 1 pound peeled frozen shrimp, thawed

1 pound lump crabmeat

1 1/4 cups Italian bread crumbs, divided

In a large pot, boil the mirlitons whole until tender when stuck with a fork, about 1 hour. Drain and cool.

Meanwhile, melt 4 tablespoons of the butter in a large skillet. Add the onion, the white parts of the green onions, and the celery and sauté until transparent. Add the garlic and sauté a minute more. Add the seasonings and lemon juice and remove from the heat.

Cut the mirlitons in half lengthwise and remove the seeds. Scoop out the flesh, leaving a shell of about 1/4-inch thickness. Add the mirliton flesh to the skillet and simmer for about 5 minutes. Stir in the shrimp and green onion tops and cook, stirring, until the shrimp turn pink. Mix in 1/2 cup Italian bread crumbs and crabmeat, tossing gently so that the crabmeat stays in chunks.

Line a greased baking sheet with mirliton shells. Stuff the shells with the seafood mixture and sprinkle each with 1 tablespoon of the remaining bread crumbs. Cut the remaining butter into small pieces and dot the tops of the mirlitons.

Bake until brown on top, about 30 minutes. Or brown under the broiler in the last few minutes of cooking. Serve immediately.

50. Turtle Gumbo

MAKES 6 SERVINGS AS AN ENTRÉE, 12 SERVINGS AS AN APPETIZER

INGREDIENTS

2 pounds boneless turtle meat, cut into 1-inch pieces

Salt and freshly ground black pepper, to taste

10 tablespoons butter, divided

5 cups water

2 medium onions

2 green bell peppers

3 celery stalks

6 large garlic cloves

1/2 cup all-purpose flour

1 1/2 cups tomato sauce

1 teaspoon Creole seasoning

1/2 teaspoon dried thyme

1/2 teaspoon Italian seasoning

3 bay leaves

1/2 teaspoon salt

1/2 teaspoon freshly ground black pepper

2 tablespoons Worcestershire sauce

1/2 teaspoon Tabasco sauce

Juice of 1 lemon

1/2 cup good-quality sherry, plus additional for serving

4 cups chopped spinach

3 tablespoons chopped flat-leaf parsley

4 hard-boiled eggs, chopped

Sprinkle the meat lightly with salt and pepper.

Heat 2 tablespoons of the butter in a large, heavy pot and, in batches, brown the meat on all sides, removing one batch to a plate to brown the next.

Return all of the meat to the pot, cover with the water, and bring to a boil. Reduce the heat to low, cover, and simmer for about 1 hour, or until the meat is fork tender. Remove the meat to the plate and strain and reserve the stock.

When the meat is cool enough to handle, shred with your fingers and chop it into a fine dice. You may want to do this in the food processor. Set aside.

In a food processor, finely chop the onion, bell pepper, celery, and garlic. Set aside.

Rinse and dry the same pot you used to cook the turtle meat. Melt the remaining butter in the pot over low heat; add the flour and cook, stirring constantly, to make a roux the color of milk chocolate, about 10 minutes. Add the chopped vegetables and cook until very wilted. Add the tomato sauce and cook about 5 minutes. Add the stock, Creole seasoning, thyme, Italian seasoning, bay leaves, salt, pepper, Worcestershire sauce, Tabasco sauce, and lemon juice. Cook, covered, over medium-low heat for 30 minutes.

Add the sherry, spinach, and parsley and cook another 10 minutes. Remove the bay leaves and stir in the eggs.

Serve in bowls and pass extra sherry.

51. Rice and Beans with Fried Eggs

Servings: 4

INGREDIENTS

3/4 cup long-grain white rice

Kosher salt

2 tablespoon canola oil

1 small yellow onion, cut into small dice

1/2 medium red bell pepper, seeded and diced

2 large cloves of garlic, minced

1/2 teaspoon ground cumin

1/4 cup canned tomato sauce

15-ounce can of pinto beans, drained and rinsed

3 tablespoons Salsa Lizano

Freshly ground black pepper

8 large eggs

2 tablespoons chopped fresh cilantro

DIRECTIONS

Put the rice, a big pinch of salt, and 1-1/2 cups of water in a 3-quart saucepan. Bring to a boil over medium-high heat, reduce the heat to low, cover, and cook until the rice has absorbed the water and is tender about 15 minutes. Remove from the heat and set aside with the lid on.

Meanwhile, heat 1 tablespoon of the oil in a 4-quart saucepan over medium heat. Add the onion, bell pepper, garlic, and a pinch of salt; cook, stirring occasionally until softened, about 3 minutes. Add the cumin and cook until fragrant, about 30 seconds. Add the tomato sauce and stir for 1 minute.

Add the beans and 1 cup of water and simmer until the liquid reduces to the level of the beans, about 4 minutes.

Add the rice to the beans and mix well. Stir in the Salsa Lizano and season to taste with salt and pepper. Keep warm.

Heat the remaining 1 tablespoon of oil in a 12-inch non-stick skillet over medium heat, swirling the pan to coat evenly. Gently crack the eggs into the pan. Season with salt and pepper, cover, and cook until the yolks' edges have just begun to set, 2 to 3 minutes. Separate the eggs with the edge of a spatula.

To serve, put a heaping spoonful of the rice and beans on a plate and slide 2 eggs on top. Sprinkle with the cilantro.

Serve with Jícama, Avocado, Radish & Orange Salad with Cilantro, or a simple green salad.

52. Huevos Rancheros Breakfast Casserole

Servings: 8

Preparation time: 25 minutes

Cooking Time: 1 hour

INGREDIENTS

1 package pinto bean and long-grain rice mix

2 tablespoons unsalted butter

2 tablespoons vegetable or canola oil, or as needed

12 corn tortillas

15-ounce can of enchilada sauce

½ teaspoon ground cumin

½ teaspoon garlic powder

½ teaspoon chili powder

2 cups shredded cheddar or Mexican blend cheese

8 large eggs

Kosher salt and freshly ground pepper to taste

To serve:

1 cup salsa

1 avocado, thinly sliced

½ cup sour cream

4 scallions, trimmed and sliced

½ cup cilantro leaves

DIRECTIONS

Preheat the oven to 425°F. Grease a 13 x 9-inch baking dish, or spray with non-stick cooking spray. Place the beans and rice mix in a medium-sized saucepan with 2 ½ cups of water and the butter.

Bring to a simmer over medium-high heat, then reduce the heat slightly, cover and keep at a simmer for about 20 to 25 minutes, until the rice is tender, making sure to stir occasionally. Remove from the heat, and let stand for 5 minutes. Remove the lid and fluff with a fork, and set aside.

While the rice and beans are cooking, prepare the tortillas. Place paper towels on a work surface. Heat 1 teaspoon of the oil in a skillet over medium-high heat, and cook the tortillas one at a time, for about 1 to 2 minutes on each side, or until just crisp and browned in spots.

As they are cooked, transfer them to paper towels. Add more oil, 1 teaspoon at a time as needed until all of the tortillas are cooked.

Combine the enchilada sauce with the cumin, garlic powder, and chili powder. Layer half the tortillas in the bottom of the prepared pan, overlapping them to cover the bottom of the pan. Drizzle over half of the enchilada sauce, then sprinkle over half of the cheese. Spread the bean and rice mixture over the cheese. Repeat layering the tortillas, enchilada sauce, and cheese.

Use a spoon and your fingers to create 8 evenly spaced little wells in the top of the casserole, breaking holes through the top layer of tortillas so that the eggs have enough room to sink into their indentations. Use the spoon and your fingers to create these wells, making them about 1 inch deep. Crack the eggs carefully into the wells, and season them with salt and pepper.

Bake until the whites of the eggs are set, but the yolks are still loose and runny about 25 minutes.

Serve the eggs with salsa, avocado, sour cream, scallions, and cilantro leaves. You can divide everything over the top of the baked casserole, or spoon out individual portions and let everyone top their plate as they wish.

53. Mango and Bean Breakfast Burrito Bowl

Preparation Time: 15 Minutes

Cooking Time: 45 Minutes

Servings: 4

INGREDIENTS

1 batch of long-grain green rice, cooked

15-ounce can of pinto beans, rinsed and drained

2 ripe mangos, diced

1 avocado, diced or sliced

1 red bell pepper, diced

1 cup corn, grilled, raw or sautéed

½ cup diced cilantro

¼ cup diced red onion

1 jalapeño, sliced

Dressings:

Jalapeño cilantro mango

Cilantro lime

Jalapeño cashew sauce

DIRECTIONS

When you are done, divide the rice between four bowls, then divide beans, mango, avocado, red bell pepper, corn, cilantro, red onion, and jalapeño slices evenly between the bowls.

Serve with lime wedges.

54. Slow Cooker Stuffed Bell Peppers

Total Time: 60 Minutes

Servings: 4

INGREDIENTS

2 teaspoons avocado oil

1 sweet onion, diced

2 celery, sliced

4 cloves garlic, minced

1 tablespoon chili powder

2 teaspoons cumin

1 1/2 teaspoons dried oregano

2 cups long-grain white rice, cooked and cooled

1 cup frozen corn kernels

1 tomato, diced

1 can of pinto beans, rinsed and drained

1 chipotle pepper in adobo

salt

5 bell peppers

1 can enchilada sauce

pepper jack cheese, shredded

DIRECTIONS

Heat oil in a large skillet over medium-high heat. Add the onion and celery and cook, stirring often, for about 5 minutes. Add the garlic and cook for 30 seconds or so and remove from heat.

Add the spices and stir well. In a large bowl add the rice, beans, corn, tomato, chipotle pepper, 1/4 cup of enchilada sauce, and onion mixture. Stir well and season with salt and pepper.

Cut the tops from the bell peppers and remove the seeds and ribs. Fill with the rice mixture, packing lightly. I filled mine halfway, added a small amount of cheese, and then finished filling. Don't put cheese on top yet. Place the filled peppers in the slow cooker.

Add about 1/2 inch of water to the crock being careful not to get water in the peppers. Cook on low for about 4 hours. About 15 minutes before they are done add a layer of cheese to each pepper and let finish cooking.

Serve the peppers with the rest of the enchilada sauce and extra cheese if desired. Enjoy!

55. Mixed Bean and Rice Dip

Servings: 10 to 12

INGREDIENTS

For the dip:

15-ounce can of pinto beans, rinsed and drained

15-ounce can of black beans, rinsed and drained

15-ounce can of navy beans, rinsed and drained

1 cup cooked white rice

1 cup diced tomato

1/2 cup diced onion

3 cups grated Cheddar-Monterey Jack blend

2 tablespoons finely diced pickled jalapeño

1/2 teaspoon ground cumin

1/2 teaspoon garlic powder

1/8 teaspoon cayenne pepper

Kosher salt and freshly ground pepper

For serving:

Tortilla chips

Sour cream

Salsa

DIRECTIONS

Preheat the oven to 400°.

In a large bowl, combine the beans, rice, tomato, onion, 2 cups of cheese, jalapeño, and spices. Season generously with kosher salt and pepper.

Pour into a greased 10-inch cast-iron skillet or round baking dish. Cover with aluminum foil and cook for 30 minutes.

Remove from the oven and take off the aluminum foil. Sprinkle the remaining 1 cup of cheese over the top and continue to bake until the cheese is melted, about 5 - 10 more minutes.

Serve warm with tortilla chips, sour cream, and salsa.

56. Pinto Beans and Rice Balls

Servings: 30

INGREDIENTS

1 can of pinto beans rinsed and drained

1 cup cooked long-grain white rice

1 egg

1/4 teaspoon kosher salt more to taste

1/4 teaspoon cumin

pinch of cayenne more to taste

1-2 tablespoons olive oil

Smoky Chipotle Dipping Sauce

DIRECTIONS

Place the rinsed beans in a large mixing bowl. Mash with a potato masher until they form a paste. Add the rice, cumin, and cayenne. Stir to combine and taste.

Add the egg and work with your hands or a large spoon to combine well.

Use a small scoop or a spoon to form the balls and then gently round them with your fingertips. Form all of the balls and place them on a large plate or cutting board. In a large skillet over medium-high heat, warm about a tablespoon of oil. Cook the balls in the skillet, until they are lightly browned on each side. This took a couple of minutes on each side, turning them 2-3 times each.

If you aren't familiar with cooking things in batches, here is a tip.

Start placing your rice balls in the pan, at the outer edge, next to the handle. Go clockwise around the pan and then fill in the middle.

After the balls are browned, remove them from the pan and place them on a clean plate. Tent loosely with foil to keep warm. Cook the remaining half of the balls and then serve warm. Enjoy!

57. Deep-Fried Beans, Rice, and Sausage Balls

INGREDIENTS:

1 cup cooked long-grain rice

1 cup of pinto beans, cooked until creamy

4 thinly sliced green onions

4 Tablespoons finely chopped sausage

1 cup plus 2 tablespoons dried breadcrumbs in all

2 teaspoons hot sauce - your choice

2 eggs in all

1 cup all-purpose flour

1/2 cup milk

oil for deep frying

Creole Dipping Sauce:

1-part Mayonnaise

1-part Creole mustard

DIRECTIONS:

Mix rice, beans, onions, sausage, and 2 tablespoons of breadcrumbs. Sprinkle on hot sauce, then stir in one egg to form a tight batter.

Whisk milk and remaining egg to make an egg wash.

Form small balls from beans, rice, and sausage mixture. Roll in flour, then coat with egg wash and roll in the remaining breadcrumbs.

Heat oil to 360 degrees F and fry until golden brown. Drain on paper towels and serve immediately with Creole Dipping Sauce, or your favorite dipping sauce.

Creole Dipping Sauce: Mix one-part mayonnaise with one-part Creole Mustard, and serve with the beans and rice balls.

58. Long-grain Rice and pinto bean

Preparation time: 30 minutes

Cooking time: 10 to 30 minutes

Servings: 4

INGREDIENTS

50ml/2fl oz. vegetable oil

1 onion, finely chopped

300ml/10½ oz. long-grain rice

400ml/14½ oz. water

400ml/14½ oz. coconut milk

400g/14¼oz Can pinto beans, rinsed and drained

3 tablespoons fresh thyme

salt and freshly ground black pepper

fresh coriander, to garnish

DIRECTIONS

Heat the oil in a frying pan and fry the onion until translucent.

Add the rice, stir well and add the water and coconut milk. Bring to the boil.

Add the pinto beans and thyme, simmer, and cover, for about 20 minutes until the rice is cooked. Season with salt and freshly ground black pepper.

Serve garnished with the coriander.

59. Lime chicken with egg-fried long-grain rice

Preparation time: 30 minutes

Cooking time: 10 to 30 minutes

Servings: 2

INGREDIENTS

For The Chicken

2 skinless chicken breasts

2 tablespoon sesame oil

2 teaspoon vegetable oil

2 tablespoon soy sauce

2 garlic cloves, finely chopped

½ lemon, grated zest, and juice

salt and freshly ground black pepper

1 tablespoon clear honey

For The Rice

2 tablespoon groundnut oil

2-3 teaspoon sesame oil

2 free-range eggs, lightly beaten

splash soy sauce

2 spring onions, finely chopped

50g/2oz pinto beans, cooked

150g/5oz long-grain rice, cooked

salt and freshly ground black pepper

3-4 tablespoons chopped coriander

lime wedges, to serve

DIRECTIONS

To butterfly, the chicken breasts lay them on a board and use a sharp knife to make a cut parallel to the chopping board three-quarters of the way through each breast.

Open each chicken breast out so you have two large, thinner chicken breasts.

Place them in a bowl with one tablespoon of the sesame oil, the vegetable oil, soy sauce, garlic, lemon zest, and juice.

Season with salt and freshly ground black pepper and mix to combine. In a separate bowl, mix the honey with the remaining sesame oil.

Heat a griddle pan over medium-high heat until smoking then lay the chicken on the griddle and cook for 2-3 minutes on each side, brushing it once or twice with the honey and sesame mixture.

When it's done the chicken should be char-grilled on the outside and completely cooked through. Leave to rest for 2-3 minutes.

Meanwhile, for the rice, heat a wok over high heat then add the groundnut and one teaspoon of the sesame oil. When the oil starts to shimmer add the eggs and cook, stirring all the time, for 1-2 minutes or until they're scrambled.

Push the eggs to the side of the pan and add a little more sesame oil, the soy sauce, spring onions, and pinto beans and cook for one minute then add the rice and season with salt and freshly ground black pepper.

Cook, stirring continuously, for 3-4 minutes, or until warmed through. Stir through the coriander.

To serve, spoon the rice onto plates. Cut the chicken on the diagonal into thin strips and place it on top of the rice. Top with a wedge of lime.

60. Long-grain Rice Hoppin' John

Preparation time: 30 minutes

Cooking time: 30 minutes to 1 hour

Servings: 4

INGREDIENTS

2 tablespoon vegetable oil

300g/10½oz cooked and shredded bacon

1 green pepper, finely chopped

1 red pepper, finely chopped

1 red onion, finely chopped

3 celery sticks, finely chopped

4 garlic cloves, crushed

1 teaspoon dried chili flakes

2 bay leaves

1 litre/1¾ pint of chicken or vegetable stock

400g/14oz can pinto beans, drained and rinsed

225g/8oz long-grain rice

2 tablespoon Creole or all-purpose seasoning

salt and freshly ground black pepper

To serve

a handful of flat-leaf parsley leaves, finely chopped

bunch spring onions, finely chopped

DIRECTIONS

Heat the oil in a large pan over medium heat.

Add bacon to the pan and fry until crispy. Remove with a slotted spoon and drain on kitchen paper.

Add the onion, peppers, celery, garlic, chili flakes, bay leaves, Creole seasoning, salt, and pepper to the pan and sauté on a low to medium heat until softened.

Pour in the stock and bring to a boil.

Add the rice, beans, and bacon, and stir well. Cover and simmer for 20 minutes, or until the rice is tender and most of the liquid has been absorbed.

Divide between serving bowls, sprinkle with the parsley and spring onions and serve.

61. Mexican-Inspired Pinto Beans and Rice

Preparation Time: 25 minutes

Cooking Time: 20 minutes

Servings: 8

INGREDIENTS

1 tablespoon Chicken Bouillon

3 tablespoons tomato paste

1 teaspoon ground coriander seeds

1 teaspoons salt

½ teaspoons garlic powder

¼ teaspoons pepper

3½ cups water

2 cups long-grain white rice, rinsed using a mesh strainer

1 red bell pepper, stemmed, seeded, and diced

¼ cup finely chopped red onion

1 jalapeño, stemmed, seeded, and finely diced

2 tablespoons finely chopped cilantro

15-ounce can of pinto beans, drained and rinsed

DIRECTIONS

To a pot, add Chicken Base, tomato paste, coriander, salt, garlic powder, and pepper; whisk to combine.

Gradually whisk in water, add rice and stir to combine. Place a pot over medium-high heat and bring to a boil, stirring occasionally.

Reduce heat to medium-low, cover. Continue to cook until liquid has been absorbed, stirring occasionally, about 12-15 minutes. Remove from heat and let stand covered for a few minutes.

Place rice in a large bowl and add bell pepper, onion, jalapeño, and cilantro; stir to combine.

Gently stir in beans and serve.

62. Pinto Beans and Rice with Cilantro

Preparation Time: 5 minutes

Cooking Time: 25 minute

Servings 6

INGREDIENTS

For the Rice:

1 cup long-grain white rice

1 tablespoon olive oil

8 oz. can of tomato sauce

1 red bell pepper cored, seeded, and quartered

1 1/2 cups chicken stock or vegetable broth

3/4 teaspoon kosher salt

1 teaspoon garlic powder

1/4 teaspoon chili powder

1/4 teaspoon cumin

1/2 cup diced tomatoes

2 tablespoons chopped cilantro for garnish

For the Beans:

15 ounces can of pinto beans drained and rinsed

1/2 cup chicken stock or vegetable broth

1 tablespoon tomato paste

3/4 teaspoon salt

3/4 teaspoon chili powder

1/2 cup pico de gallo for garnish

DIRECTIONS

For the Rice:

Heat the olive oil in a 2-quart pot over medium heat. Add the rice and stir until the rice is coated in the oil. Cook for about 5 minutes or until the rice is toasted and lightly browned.

Add all of the remaining **INGREDIENTS**.

Return the pot to the burner, and bring the contents to a boil.

Cover the pot and turn the heat to low; cook for 17 minutes.

Take the pot off the heat and let it stand, covered for 5 minutes. Remove and discard bell peppers. Stir well. Garnish with tomatoes and green onions if desired.

For the Beans:

Put all of the Ingredients in a pan over medium-high heat, and bring to a simmer. Cook for 7-10 minutes until the sauce has thickened. Taste and add more salt or chili powder if needed. You can also add a bit more chicken stock if the sauce gets too thick for your liking. Garnish with pico de gallo if desired.

63. Spanish Pinto Beans & Rice

Preparation Time 10 minutes

Cooking Time 25 minutes

Servings 2

INGREDIENTS

FOR THE RICE

2 cups vegetable broth 475 ml

1 cup long-grain rice 190 grams

1/4 teaspoons saffron threads .17 grams

pinch sea salt

dash black pepper

FOR THE BEANS

2 tablespoons extra virgin olive oil 30 ml

1 small onion

4 cloves garlic

1 carrot

1 green bell pepper

1 teaspoon sweet smoked Spanish paprika 2.30 grams

1/2 teaspoon ground cumin 1.25 grams

2 1/2 cups canned pinto beans 400 grams

1 cup vegetable broth 240 ml

pinch sea salt

dash black pepper

a handful of finely chopped fresh parsley

DIRECTIONS

Add 2 cups vegetable broth into a saucepan, pinch in 1/4 teaspoons saffron threads, and season with sea salt & freshly cracked black pepper, heat with a high heat

Meanwhile, add 1 cup of long-grain rice into a sieve and rinse under cold running water, until the water runs clear underneath the sieve

Once the broth comes to a boil, add the rice into the pan, give it a mix and place a lid on the pan, lower to low-medium heat, and simmer until the rice is cooked.

Meanwhile, heat a large fry-pan with medium heat and add 2 tablespoons extra virgin olive oil, after 2 minutes add 1 small onion finely diced, 1 green bell pepper finely chopped, 1 carrot, and 4 cloves garlic roughly minced, mix the vegetable continuously with the olive oil

After 4 minutes and the vegetables are lightly sautéed, add in 1 teaspoon sweet smoked Spanish paprika and 1/2 teaspoons ground cumin, quickly mix, then add in 2 1/2 cups canned pinto beans and season with sea salt & black pepper, gently mix until well mixed, then add in 1 cup vegetable broth and simmer on a medium heat

Once the rice is cooked through, remove the rice from the heat, let it sit for 3 to 4 minutes with the lid on, then remove the lid and fluff up the rice with a fork, and transfer the rice into the serving dishes

Grab the simmering beans and add them into the serving dish next to the rice, sprinkle with freshly chopped parsley, and enjoy!

64. One-Pot Rice and Beans

Servings: 4 servings

Total Time: 30 minutes

INGREDIENTS

2 tablespoons olive oil

1 yellow onion, chopped

1 $\frac{3}{4}$ cups chicken or vegetable stock or water

1 teaspoon salt

1 cup long-grain rice

15.5-ounce can of pinto beans

Lime wedges or cilantro leaves, for garnish

DIRECTIONS

In a large saucepan or Dutch oven with a tight-fitting lid, warm the olive oil over medium heat. Add onion and sauté until translucent, about 3 minutes. Add the stock, cover, and bring to a boil.

Add the salt, rice, and beans. Stir just to combine, then cover.

Turn the heat down as low as it will go, then let simmer, undisturbed, for 18 to 20 minutes. Remove from heat and let sit for 4 minutes, then fluff with a fork.

Season to taste with salt and pepper, then garnish with lime or cilantro as you wish.

65. Southern Pinto Beans and Rice

Preparation Time: 5 minutes

Cooking Time: 4 hours

Servings: 6 cups

INGREDIENTS

1 lb. dried pinto beans

8 cups water or broth

2 tablespoons salt, for overnight soaking; table salt

2 tablespoons onion powder or 1 cup fresh, diced onion

2 tablespoons garlic powder

2 cups long-grain rice, cooked

1 smoked ham hock

salt and pepper to taste

DIRECTIONS

Put beans in a large Dutch oven with onion and garlic powder.

Cook on low heat, uncovered, for 3-4 hours or until tender; check liquid level frequently; add more if needed; when tender, taste for seasonings and adjust accordingly

1 lb. dried pinto beans,8 cups water or broth,2 tablespoons onion powder,2 tablespoons garlic powder,1 smoked ham hock

66. Pinto Beans and Rice and Sausage

Preparation Time: 20 minutes

Cooking Time: 105 minutes

Servings: 6 servings

INGREDIENTS

1 pound dried pinto beans

6 cups water

1 ham hock, or a meaty leftover ham bone

1 medium onion, chopped

3 cloves garlic, minced

1 1/2 teaspoons salt

1-pound andouille smoked sausage, or similar smoked sausage, sliced

14.5-ounce can of tomatoes, diced

4-ounce can of mild green chile peppers

1/2 teaspoon red pepper flakes, crushed

4 cups cooked white rice, long-grain, or quick grits, hot boiled

DIRECTIONS

The night before put the pinto beans in a large bowl or pot and cover with water to a depth of about 3 inches above the beans. Let them stand for 8 hours or overnight. Drain well.

Combine the soaked and drained beans with water, ham hock, onion, and garlic in a large saucepan or Dutch oven over high heat; bring to a boil. Cover and reduce the heat to medium; cook the beans for 45 minutes, or until the beans are tender.

Add the salt, sliced sausage, tomatoes, mild chile peppers, and crushed red pepper flakes, if desired. Cover, reduce heat to low, and simmer for 1 hour, stirring occasionally.

Remove the ham hock and remove the meat from the bone. Shred the ham with a fork or chop. Return the ham to the bean mixture.

Serve the pinto beans over hot cooked rice.

67. Gallopinto (Nicaraguan Rice and Beans)

Preparation Time: 45 minutes

Total Time: 24 hours

Servings: 8 servings

INGREDIENTS

For the beans

1 (16-ounce) bag dried Pinto beans

Salt

7 garlic cloves, peeled

For the rice

1/4 cup vegetable oil, divided

1 medium yellow onion, finely chopped

1 1/2 cups long-grain white rice

3 cups water or low-sodium chicken broth

1/2 green bell pepper, cored and seeded

DIRECTIONS

For the beans:

Spread beans out on a rimmed baking sheet. Pick out any debris and broken beans. Transfer beans to a colander and rinse under cold running water. Place rinsed beans in a large pot and cover with cold water; let soak for 30 minutes.

Bring to boil over high heat. Reduce heat to medium and simmer beans for 30 minutes. Turn off heat, cover beans, and let rest for 1 hour. Bring beans back up to boil over high heat. Add 2 teaspoons salt and garlic, reduce heat to medium, and simmer until beans are tender 30 to 60 minutes.

For the rice:

Heat 2 tablespoons oil in a large heavy-bottomed saucepan over medium heat until shimmering. Add 2/3 of onion and cook, stirring, until softened and translucent, about 5 minutes.

Add rice and cook, stirring, until grains are shiny and evenly coated with oil, 2 to 3 minutes. Add water or broth and 1 1/2 teaspoons salt, increase heat to high, and bring to a boil. Place bell pepper on top of rice.

Boil rice without stirring until most of the liquid has evaporated and you can see small bubbles bursting on the surface of the rice. Immediately reduce the heat to the lowest setting, cover, and cook for 15 minutes.

Remove and discard bell pepper. Fluff rice with chopsticks or fork, then let cool and refrigerate for 1 day.

For the gallopinto:

Heat the remaining 2 tablespoons of oil in a large saucepan over medium-high heat until shimmering. Add remaining onion and cook, stirring, until softened and translucent, about 5 minutes.

Add rice and 2 cups beans to skillet and cook, stirring, until rice is evenly coated. Continue to cook, stirring, to allow flavors to meld and the mixture to become slightly crisp, about 10 minutes. Cover and cook over low heat for an additional 10 minutes.

68. Bean sauce & tomatoes over rice

Servings: 6 servings

INGREDIENTS

1 cup pinto beans, soaked

2 Serrano chilies, seeded & chopped

½ tablespoon Ginger, grated

1 each Bay leaf

¼ teaspoon Turmeric

4 cups Water

1⅓ cup Stock

¼ cup Cilantro

Salt & pepper

2 tablespoons Pecans, chopped & toasted

2 tablespoons Olive oil

4 Tomatoes, diced

1 teaspoon Chili powder

1 tablespoon fresh marjoram

1 teaspoon Maple syrup

5 cups Water

$1\frac{1}{2}$ cup Long-grain Rice

2 Carrots, shredded

1 each 3" cinnamon stick

$\frac{1}{2}$ tablespoon Olive oil

DIRECTIONS

Cook beans for $1\frac{1}{2}$ to 2 hours, until the beans are tender. Discard bay leaf &

SAUCE:

Combine drained beans, chilies, ginger, bay leaf, turmeric & water in a large pot.

Bring to a boil, reduce heat, cover & cook.

Place beans, stock & cilantro in a food processor & pulse into a chunky sauce. Season, add pecans & reheat slightly.

TOMATOES:

Combine tomatoes, chili powder, marjoram & syrup in a sauté pan. Season with salt & pepper & stir-fry over moderate heat till the tomato begins to caramelize, about 10 minutes. Keep warm on low heat.

RICE:

Boil water, and stir in rice, carrots & cinnamon. Cook until the rice is tender, 10 to 12 minutes if using white rice. Drain & discard cinnamon & rinse briefly under running water.

Return to pan & toss with oil.

To serve, spoon rice onto warm plates, top with bean sauce & scatter with tomatoes.

69. Cajun pinto beans

Servings: 8

INGREDIENTS

1 each Small bag of pinto beans, washed and picked through

¼ cup Flour

¼ cup Bacon grease

1 large Onion, chopped

6 cloves Garlic, chopped

½ cup Celery, chopped

1 each Bay leaf

¼ cup Chili powder

2 tablespoons ground cumin

1 can of tomatoes with chilies

Salt to taste

2 pounds Ham hock or salt pork

Chopped cilantro

2 cups Long-grain rice, cooked

DIRECTIONS

Pick through pinto beans and wash. Soak 1 small bag of pinto beans overnight in cold water and 1 tablespoon of baking soda. Rinse beans and cook for 1 hour. Change the water and add 1 tablespoon of baking soda again. Cook for another hour or two and change the water for the last time, add baking soda, and cook till done.

Fry ¼ cup flour and ¼ cup bacon grease into the dark roux.

Add and stir the following until wilted: 1 large chopped onion, 5 or 6 cloves chopped garlic, ½ cup chopped celery, 1 bay leaf, and cilantro.

Add chili powder, cumin, and tomatoes with chilies and salt to taste.

May be cooked with ham hock or salt pork.

Using this roux adds a truly great flavor to pinto beans.

Serve with long-grain rice.

70. Rice & beans with cheese

Servings: 5

INGREDIENTS

1⅓ cup Water

1 cup Shredded Carrots

1 teaspoon instant chicken bouillon

¼ teaspoon Salt

15 ounces Can Pinto Beans, drained

8 ounces Plain lo-fat Yogurt

½ cup Shredded Low-fat Cheddar cheese

⅔ cup Long-grain Rice

½ cup Sliced Green Onions

½ teaspoon Ground Coriander

1 teaspoon Hot Pepper Sauce

1 cup Low-fat Cottage Cheese

1 tablespoon Snipped fresh parsley

DIRECTIONS

In a large saucepan combine water, rice, carrots, green onions, bouillon granules, coriander, salt, and bottled hot pepper sauce.

Bring to boiling; reduce heat. Cover and simmer for 15 minutes or till rice is tender and water is absorbed.

Stir in pinto or navy beans, cottage cheese, yogurt, and parsley.

Spoon into a 10x6x2" baking dish.

Bake, covered, in a 350 degrees F. oven for 20-25 minutes or till heated through. Sprinkle with cheddar cheese. Bake, uncovered, for 3-5 minutes more or till cheese melts.

71. Pinto Beans and Saffron Rice

Servings: 4

INGREDIENTS

Beans

3 cups dried pinto beans

1/2 stick butter

1/3 cup lard

1/2 cup sofrito

1 large onion diced

3 quarts water

Rice

1-1/2 cup long-grain rice

3 cups chicken broth

1/2 teaspoon saffron threads

1-1/2 teaspoon kosher salt

1/2 cup water

1 tablespoon butter

Vinegar Hot pepper sauce

DIRECTIONS

Wash the beans and remove all foreign objects such as stones and bad beans.

Dice the onions.

Add the onion, beans, sofrito, water, and butter.

Let it heat for 4 minutes and add the lard.

Cover and boil for 15 minutes stir, cover again, and reduce heat by half. Cook till beans are tender and then add salt.

Melt the butter and add the rice. Stir well and add the saffron, broth, and water.

Boil the rice stirring occasionally then when the liquids are absorbed cover and remove from heat don't disturb for 20 minutes.

Serve with the beans over the rice. Add the vinegar and hot pepper sauce.

72. Taco Seasoning rice with pinto beans

Servings: 6 Servings

INGREDIENTS

2 cups Water

8 ounces of Tomato sauce

1 pack taco seasoning mix

1 cup Corn

½ cup Green pepper -- chopped

½ teaspoon Oregano

⅛ teaspoon Garlic powder

1 cup long-grain rice

16 ounces Pinto beans, canned

DIRECTIONS

In a medium saucepan, combine all Ingredients, except rice & beans.

Bring mixture to a boil over medium heat. Stir in rice and beans.

When mixture boils again, stir, then reduce heat to medium-low, cover, and simmer until most of the liquid has cooked out, 45 minutes to 1 hour.

Remove from heat, and set aside covered for 5 minutes.

Mix well.

73. Indian pumpkin rice and beans

Servings: 8

INGREDIENTS

1 tablespoon Canola oil

1 medium Yellow onion; chopped

2 Clove garlic; minced

2 cups Pumpkin cubes

2 teaspoons Curry powder

½ teaspoon Black pepper

½ teaspoon Salt

¼ teaspoon Ground cloves

1½ cup long-grain white rice

1 cup Coarsely chopped kale or spinach

15 ounces Cooked pinto beans; drained and rinsed

DIRECTIONS

In a large saucepan heat the oil over medium heat.

Add the onion and garlic and cook, stirring, for 5 minutes until the onion is translucent. Stir in the pumpkin, curry, pepper, salt, and clove, and cook for 1 minute more.

Add 3 cups of water and the rice, cover, and bring to a simmer. Cook over medium-low heat for about 15 minutes.

Stir in the kale and beans and cook for about 5 minutes more.

Fluff the rice and turn off the heat. Let stand for 10 to 15 minutes before serving.

74. Mexican Cowboy Beans

Servings: 6

INGREDIENTS

½ lb. Pinto beans, dried
1 Onion, white, large
3 cloves Garlic, crushed
2 sprigs Cilantro
¼ cup Vegetable stock or water
6 oz. Vegan chorizo
2 Serrano chilies, minced
1 Tomato, large, diced

DIRECTIONS

Soak beans in water overnight.
The next day, strain them and place them in a large pot. Pour enough water into the pot to fill ¾ of the way.
Cut your onion in half. Place ½ the onion, cilantro sprigs, and 3 garlic cloves into the pot with the beans. Reserve the other half of the onion.
Bring water to a simmer and let beans cook until almost tender, approximately 1 ½ hours.
While the beans are cooking heat a large sauté pan to medium-high heat. Add chorizo and sauté until slightly browned about 4 minutes. While the chorizo is cooking, dice the other half of the onion.
Remove chorizo from the pan and set it aside. Add ¼ cup of water, diced onion, and Serrano peppers to the sauté pan.
Sweat onion and chilies until tender and translucent about 4 - 5 minutes. Add tomato and let cook for 7-8 minutes more or until the tomato has broken down and released all of its juices.

Add this mixture and the chorizo to the pot of beans and let simmer for 20 more minutes or until beans are completely tender. Season to taste with salt and pepper.

Before serving, remove the half onion, cilantro sprig, and garlic cloves from the beans. Season with salt and pepper

75. Caribbean Feast

INGREDIENTS

JERK JACKFRUIT

3 Cans of Young Jack Fruit in brine, drained & diced
1 tablespoon Coconut Oil
3 Spring Onions, finely sliced
3 Cloves Garlic, minced
1/2 Scotch Bonnet Chili
Thumb sized piece of ginger, minced
1 Yellow Pepper, deseeded & cubed
1 cup/200g canned pinto beans
1 tablespoon All Spice
2 teaspoon Ground Cinnamon
3 tablespoons Soy Sauce
5 tablespoons Tomato Purée
4 tablespoons Coconut Sugar
1 cup/240ml Pineapple Juice
Juice 1 lime
1 tablespoon Fresh Thyme Leaves
2 teaspoon Sea Salt
1 teaspoon Cracked Black Pepper

RICE & PEAS

1 Can Kidney Beans, liquid reserved
1 Can Coconut Milk
3 tablespoons Fresh Thyme
Pinch Sea Salt & Black Pepper

1 & 1/2 cups/340g Long Grain Rice, rinsed
Vegetable stock, if needed.

FRIED PLANTAIN

2 Plantain, peeled & cut into cm discs
2 tablespoons Vita Coca Coconut Oil
2 tablespoons Coconut Sugar
Pinch Salt & Pepper

MANGO SALAD

1/2 Fresh Mango, peeled and cubed
1 teaspoon Fresh Chili, chopped fine
Handful Fresh Coriander
Juice of Half a Lime
Fresh Mixed Salad

DIRECTIONS

First up place a large casserole dish or frying pan over medium heat. Add the coconut oil followed by the onion, garlic, ginger, chili & yellow pepper. Allow the mix to soften for 3 minutes before adding the spices & cooking for 2 more minutes. Add a pinch of seasoning.
Add the jackfruit to the pan and stir well, cook the mix for 3-4 minutes.
Next, add the coconut sugar & the beans. Keep stirring then add the soy sauce, tomato purée & pineapple juice. Turn the

heat down low & add the lime juice plus some chopped fresh thyme leaves.

Pop the lid on and allow the jackfruit to cook for around 12-15 minutes.

For the rice, add the Ingredients to a saucepan and pop the lid on. place the pan over low heat and allow the rice to absorb all the liquid until it's light & fluffy. this should take 10-12 minutes. if your rice gets too dry before it has cooked, add some water or vegetable stock.

next up, is the plantain. preheat a non-stick frying pan over medium heat & add the coconut oil, when hot add the plantain wedges, and cook on both sides for 3-4 minutes until caramelized & golden. season with coconut sugar, salt & pepper.

For the salad, simply mix all the Ingredients in a small mixing bowl.

serve everything together, enjoy.

76. Jamaican Jerk Jackfruit & Beans with Rice

Preparation Time: 10 minutes

Cooking Time: 25 minutes

Servings: 2

INGREDIENTS

1 onion

2 garlic cloves

1 chili

2 vine tomatoes

2 teaspoon Jamaican jerk seasoning

400g Can of kidney beans

400g Can of jackfruit

200ml coconut milk

150g white long-grain rice

50g baby leaf spinach

Sea salt

Freshly ground pepper

1 tablespoon olive oil

300ml boiling water

DIRECTIONS

Peel and finely chop the onion. Peel and grate the garlic cloves. Halve the chili, flicking out the seeds and membrane for less heat, and finely chop. Roughly chop the tomatoes.

Pour1 tablespoon of oil into a large pan and bring to medium heat. Slide in the onions and a good pinch of salt and pepper. Fry for 4-5 minutes, stirring occasionally, till softened and slightly colored. Stir in the garlic, chili, and 2 teaspoons Jamaican jerk seasoning and continue to fry for a further 2 minutes

Tip the chopped tomatoes into the pan. Drain the kidney beans and jackfruit and add them to the pan. Pour in the coconut milk. Combine well and bring to a boil, then partly cover with a lid and simmer gently for 20 minutes During the cooking time, use a wooden spoon now and then to break up the jackfruit chunks a little.

Tip the rice into a sieve and give it a good rinse under cold water. Tip into a small pan and add 300ml boiling water and a pinch of salt. Pop on a lid and bring to a boil, then turn right down and very gently simmer for 8 minutes, till all the water has been absorbed. Take the rice off the heat and leave it to steam in the pan, covered, for 10 minutes

Stir the spinach into the jackfruit and beans till wilted. Have a taste of the sauce and add more salt if needed.

Spoon the rice into a couple of deep bowls and top with generous ladlefuls of the jackfruit curry and serve.

77. Rice Pilaf with Bean, Fruits, and Nuts

Preparation Time: 10 minutes

Cooking Time: 45 minutes

INGREDIENTS

1 1/2 cups long-grain rice

1 tablespoon neutral vegetable oil

1 medium onion, finely chopped

1 to 2 small fresh hot chili peppers, sliced

2/3 cup raisins or dried cranberries, or a combination

1/3 cup cooked pinto beans

1/3 cup finely chopped dried apricots

1/4 teaspoon turmeric

1/2 teaspoon cinnamon

1/4 teaspoon ground or fresh nutmeg

1/2 teaspoon dried basil

1/4 cup orange juice

2 teaspoons agave nectar

1 to 2 tablespoons lemon or lime juice, to taste

1/2 cup toasted cashews

Salt and freshly ground pepper to taste

DIRECTIONS

Combine the rice with 4 cups of water in a saucepan. Bring to a gentle boil, then lower the heat, cover, and simmer gently for 30 minutes, or until the water is absorbed.

Once the rice is done, heat the oil in a large skillet. Add the onion and chili peppers and sauté over medium heat until golden.

Stir in the rice and all the remaining ingredients except the nuts, salt, and pepper. cook over low heat, stirring frequently, for about 8 to 10 minutes, allowing the flavors to blend.

Stir in the nuts, season with salt and pepper, and serve.

78. Beans and rice cha cha cha bowl

Servings: 6

INGREDIENTS

2 tablespoons Olive oil

2 cloves garlic, minced

1 cup Sliced onion

1 cup Peeled, sliced celery

1 cup Sliced carrots

1 teaspoon Chili powder

$\frac{1}{4}$ cup Canned diced green chiles

1 pound of pinto beans

2 cups cooked black beans

$\frac{1}{4}$ Onion, roughly sliced

1 Fat 263 Calories

2 cups sliced mushrooms

$\frac{1}{2}$ cup Reserve bean stock

2 tablespoons chopped cilantro

Salt and pepper to taste

3 cups cooked long-grain rice

1 tablespoon Lemon juice

2 teaspoons salt or to taste

INGREDIENTS

In a large deep saucepan heat olive oil, and sauté garlic, onion, celery, carrots, and chili powder, until onion is translucent.

Add chiles and mushrooms and sauté for 5 minutes more.

Stir in beans, bean stock, and cilantro. Season to taste.

Cover and simmer over low heat for about 10 minutes, stirring occasionally.

Serve over rice.

79. Turnip Stir Fry with Beans

Preparation Time: 10 minutes

Cooking Time: 20 minutes

Servings: 2 people

INGREDIENTS

1 tablespoon olive oil

2 purple top turnips - scrubbed, trimmed, and diced

3 cups spinach

1 15.5 oz. can pinto beans - drained and rinsed

1 tablespoon fresh ginger - finely chopped

2 cloves garlic - pressed or minced

1 tablespoon honey

1 tablespoon rice vinegar

2 tablespoon reduced-sodium soy sauce

1 cup long-grain rice - cooked, for serving

DIRECTIONS

If you need to prepare rice or whole-grain for the meal, start that before making the stir fry.

Heat olive oil in a large skillet over medium heat. Add the turnips and cook, stirring/flipping occasionally, for 8-12 minutes or until lightly browned and tender.

While the turnips are cooking, whisk together the ginger, garlic, honey, rice vinegar, and soy sauce in a small bowl. Add the spinach, beans, and sauce to the skillet. Cook for 4-6 minutes, or until the spinach is wilted and the stir fry is heated through.

Serve warm over rice.

80. Rice with lamb, dill, and beans

Servings: 8 servings

INGREDIENTS

2 tablespoons Butter

1 medium Onion; peeled and cut into 1/4-inch-thick slices

3 pounds Boneless lamb shoulder, cubed

3 cups Water

1 tablespoon salt

2 cups uncooked long-grain white rice, soaked and drained

4 cups Dill, fresh; finely cut

2 ten oz. Pinto beans

8 tablespoons butter; melted

$\frac{1}{4}$ teaspoon Saffron threads; pulverized and dissolved in 1 tablespoon. warm water

DIRECTIONS

In a heavy 3 to 4-quart casserole, with a tightly fitting lid, melt the 2 tablespoons of butter over moderate heat.

When the foam begins to subside, add the onions and, stirring frequently, cook for about 10 minutes, or until the slices are richly browned. With a slotted spoon, transfer them to a plate.

A half dozen pieces or so at a time, brown the lamb cubes in the fat remaining in the casserole, turning them with tongs or a spoon and regulating the heat so that they color deeply and evenly without burning. As they brown, transfer the cubes of lamb to the plate with the onions.

Pour the 3 cups of water into the casserole and bring to a boil over high heat, meanwhile scraping in the brown particles clinging to the bottom and sides of the pan. Return the lamb and onion to the casserole, add the salt, and reduce the heat to low.

Cover tightly and simmer for about 1 hour and 15 minutes, or until the lamb is tender and shows no resistance when pierced with the point of a small, sharp knife. Transfer the lamb, onions, and all the cooking liquid to a large bowl and set the casserole aside.

Preheat the oven to 350 degrees. Bring 6 cups of water to a boil in a 5 to 6-quart saucepan. Pour in the rice in a slow, thin stream so the water does not stop boiling. Stir once or twice, boil briskly for 5 minutes, then remove the pan from the heat, stir in the dill and beans and drain in a fine sieve.

Ladle about half of the rice mixture into the casserole and moisten it with «a cup of the lamb cooking liquid. Then with a spatula or spoon spread the rice mixture to the edges of the pan.

With a slotted spoon return the lamb and onions to the casserole and smooth them over the rice.

Then spread the remaining rice mixture on top. Combine 2 tablespoons of the melted butter with 6 tablespoons of the lamb broth and pour it over the rice. Bring the casserole to a boil over high heat.

Cover tightly and bake in the middle of the oven for 30 to 40 minutes, or until the beans are tender and the rice has absorbed all the liquid in the casserole.

To serve, spoon about a cup of the rice mixture into a small bowl, add the dissolved saffron and stir until the rice is bright yellow.

Spread about half the remaining rice on a heated platter and arrange the lamb over it. Cover the lamb with the rest of the plain rice mixture and garnish it with the saffron rice. Pour the remaining 6 tablespoons of melted butter over the top.

81. Cheesy Pinto Beans

Preparation Time: 10 minutes

Cooking Time: 10 minutes

Servings: 4

INGREDIENTS

2 cloves garlic

1 jalapeño

1 tablespoon cooking oil

2 15oz. cans pinto beans

1/4 teaspoon smoked paprika

1/4 teaspoon ground cumin

1/8 teaspoon freshly cracked black pepper

2 dashes of hot sauce

1/2 cup shredded cheddar cheese

2 servings of long-grain rice, cooked

DIRECTIONS

Mince the garlic and finely dice the jalapeño.

Add the garlic, jalapeño, and cooking oil to a pot. Sauté the garlic and jalapeño over medium heat for about one minute, or just until the garlic is very fragrant.

Add one can of pinto beans to a blender, with the liquid in the can, and purée until smooth.

Add the puréed beans and the second can of beans to the saucepot with the garlic and jalapeño. Stir to combine.

Season the beans with smoked paprika, cumin, pepper, and hot sauce. Stir to combine, then heat through over medium, stirring occasionally.

Finally, add the shredded cheddar and stir until it has melted smoothly into the beans. Taste the beans and adjust the seasoning to your liking. Serve over rice or with your favorite meal.

82. Rice and beans with basil pesto

Servings: 4 Servings

INGREDIENTS

Vegetable cooking spray

1 cup Chopped onion

1 cup uncooked long-grain rice

$13\frac{3}{4}$ ounce can of No-salt-added chicken broth

1 cup Chopped unpeeled tomato

$\frac{1}{4}$ cup Commercial pesto basil sauce

16 ounces of pinto beans

DIRECTIONS

Coat a large skillet with cooking spray, and place over medium-high heat until hot.

Add onion; sauté for 2 minutes. Add rice and broth; bring to a boil.

Reduce heat, and simmer, uncovered, for 15 minutes or until rice is done and liquid is absorbed.

Stir in tomato, pesto sauce, and beans; cook 2 minutes or until thoroughly heated.

83. Flank steak with beans and rice

Servings: 6 Servings

INGREDIENTS

1½ pounds Flank steak

3 tablespoons Vegetable oil

2 Bay leaves

5 cups Beef stock

4 tablespoons Olive oil

2 Onions; chopped

6 Garlic cloves; minced

1 tablespoon dried oregano

1 tablespoon ground cumin

2 Tomatoes; seeded, chopped

Salt; to taste

Freshly-ground black pepper; to taste

Pinto beans

Cooked long-grain white rice

2 tablespoons Vegetable oil

6 Eggs

DIRECTIONS

Season steak with salt and pepper. Heat vegetable oil in a heavy large skillet over high heat. Add steak and cook until browned on all sides. Add bay leaves and stock.

Reduce heat and simmer until steak is very tender, turning occasionally for about 2 hours.

Remove from heat and allow the meat to cool in the stock. Remove meat from the stock and shred it. Reserve 1 cup of cooking liquid; reserve the remaining cooking liquid for another use. Heat olive oil in a heavy large skillet over medium-high heat. Add onion and sauté until golden.

Add garlic, oregano, cumin, and sauté until fragrant. Add tomatoes and continue to cook until most of the liquid evaporates.

Add shredded meat and 1 cup of the reserved cooking liquid. Season to taste with salt and pepper. Arrange the beef, rice, and beans on a rectangular platter in three rows with the rice in the center.

Heat vegetable oil in a heavy large skillet over medium heat. Crack eggs into skillet. Fry until softly set. Serve atop beans, meat, and rice.

84. African Rice and Beans

Preparation Time: 15 minutes

Cooking Time: 35 minutes

Servings: 6

INGREDIENTS

½ cup red/palm / or canola oil

2-3 garlic cloves minced

1 medium onion diced

1 tablespoon smoked paprika

1 teaspoon dried thyme

½ scotch bonnet pepper or ½ teaspoon cayenne pepper

4 tomatoes diced

2 cups washed long grain rice

2 cups of cooked pinto beans

4 1/2 - 5 cups chicken broth or water

1 tablespoon salt or more to taste

1/4 cup crayfish

1 teaspoon chicken bouillon

DIRECTIONS

Heat a saucepan with oil. Then add onions, garlic, thyme, smoked paprika, and hot pepper, sauté for about a minute, and add tomatoes. Cook for about 5-7 minutes.

Stir in rice to the pan; continue stirring for about 2 minutes.

Then add beans, 4 1/2 cups of chicken stock/water, bring to a boil reduce heat, and simmer until rice is cooked, about 18 minutes or more. Adjust for salt and pepper. You have to stir occasionally to be preventing any burns.

Serve warm with chicken, stew, or vegetables

85. Tumbleweed, pinto bean, and rice salad

Servings: 6 servings

INGREDIENTS

¾ cup Dried pinto beans

1½ cup Tumbleweed greens or curly endive, or fennel tops, washed thoroughly and drained

1½ cup Cooked white long-grain rice

¾ cup Sunflower oil

3 tablespoons Herb flavored red wine vinegar

2 tablespoons chopped fresh chives

2 smalls Garlic cloves, peeled

¼ teaspoon Black pepper

⅛ teaspoon Salt

Chive blossoms for garnish

DIRECTIONS

Soak the beans overnight in water to cover. In the morning, drain the beans, rinse them under cold running water, and place them in a saucepan with fresh water to cover.

Bring to a boil over high heat, then reduce the heat and simmer for several hours until the beans are soft and the skins begin to split.

Add water when necessary to keep the beans from drying, and stir occasionally to prevent them from burning and sticking. Remove from the heat, drain, and allow to cool.

In a bowl, toss together the greens, beans, and rice. Cover and chill in the refrigerator for at least 30 minutes.

In a blender, combine the oil, vinegar, chives, garlic, pepper, and salt. Blend at high speed until the chives and garlic are finely puréed.

Pour the dressing over the salad, toss, and garnish with chive blossoms.

86. Pinto Bean, Rice, and Veggie Salad

Preparation Time: 15 minutes

Cooking Time: 15 minutes

Servings: 4

INGREDIENTS

2 cups water

1 cup uncooked long-grain rice

15-ounce can of pinto beans, rinsed and drained

1 red bell pepper

1 yellow bell pepper

5 green onions

¼ cup olive oil

¼ cup apple cider vinegar

1 tablespoon Dijon mustard

1 teaspoon ground cumin

1 large garlic clove

¾ teaspoon kosher salt

¼ teaspoon freshly ground black pepper

DIRECTIONS

Pour 2 cups of water into a medium saucepan. Bring to a boil, then add the uncooked rice, stir to combine, and return to a boil. Cover the pan, and reduce heat as low as possible.

Simmer without opening the lid for 15 minutes, until the rice is tender and the water is absorbed.

Finely chop the peppers. Thinly slice the green onions. Mince the garlic.

In a large mixing bowl, combine the cooked rice, beans, chopped red and yellow peppers, and scallions, and toss to combine.

In a small bowl or measuring cup, combine the olive oil, apple cider vinegar, mustard, cumin, garlic, salt, and black pepper, Whisk thoroughly to combine, then pour over the rice mixture.

Toss gently to coat, then either serve immediately or keep refrigerated for up to 3 days.

87. Edamame and Pinto Bean Salad

Preparation Time: 30 minutes

Cooking Time: 10 minutes

SERVINGS: 6

INGREDIENTS

FOR THE DRESSING

1/2 cup cider vinegar

1/4 cup olive oil

1 1/2 teaspoons cumin

1 teaspoon fresh minced garlic

Salt and pepper to taste

FOR THE SALAD

3 cups cooked long-grain rice, cooled

2 cups edamame beans

1 oz. can pinto beans

3/4 cup finely diced red pepper

3/4 cup fresh cilantro roughly chopped

Salt and pepper to taste

DIRECTIONS

In a bowl with a whisk, combine the olive oil, vinegar, garlic, and cumin. Whisk until well combined, taste, and season with salt and pepper. Set aside.

In a separate large bowl, add the cooked rice, edamame beans, chopped pepper, and pinto beans.

Mix and season with salt and pepper. Add the chopped cilantro.

Do not add the dressing just before serving. Add about half at first and taste.

Mix well and serve in a large bowl, garnished with more cilantro leaves.

88. Rice & bean salad with minced crudité

Servings: 4

INGREDIENTS

1¼ cup Cooked Long-grain rice

1 cup Cooked pinto beans -- rinsed and drained

2 tablespoons Chopped pecans -- roasted

2 tablespoons minced red bell pepper

2 tablespoons minced red onion

3 tablespoons minced fresh cilantro

3 tablespoons Green chili peppers, diced

⅓ cup Carrots -- minced

⅓ cup Broccoli florets -- minced

⅓ cup Cauliflower florets, Minced

Salt and pepper -- freshly Ground

2 cups Iceberg lettuce -- shredded

3 tablespoons Fat-free Italian salad

DIRECTIONS

Cook pinto beans, with a garnish of celery stalk, carrot chunk, and fennel stalk. Rinse, drain, chill.

About two to three hours before serving, combine the chilled rice and beans in a large mixing bowl. Peel a carrot and cut it into 1-inch pieces.

Finely chop, along with 5 to 6 broccoli florets and cauliflower florets, in a food processor. Add to the bowl and toss.

Dry-pan roast the pecans pieces for about 4 minutes over medium heat. Remove from heat. Let cool and then add to salad.

Mince by hand the onion, the red bell pepper, and the fresh cilantro leaves. Chop the canned chili peppers.

Add to salad and toss well. Taste and season with salt and pepper. Toss well.

Add 3 tablespoons of salad dressing. Toss. Chill. Serve on a bed of thinly shredded lettuce.

89. Bean and Rice Gumbo

Preparation Time 5 minutes

Cooking Time 20 minutes

Servings: 4

INGREDIENTS

2 cups chicken, cooked and cubed

1 cup long-grain rice, cooked

2 15-ounce cans of pinto beans, drained

4 cup chicken stock

2 tablespoon Taco Seasoning Mix

1 cup tomato sauce

Toppings:

Grated cheese

Salsa

Chopped cilantro

Chopped onion

DIRECTIONS

Place all Ingredients in a medium stockpot. Stir gently.

Cook over medium heat, simmering for about 20 minutes, stirring occasionally.

Serve with toppings.

90. Chili con Carne

INGREDIENTS

500g Ground/minced beef
1 Large onion chopped
3 cloves of Garlic
2 (15-Ounce each) Can of chopped tomatoes
A squeeze of tomato purée
1 teaspoon of chili powder
1 teaspoon of ground cumin
dash of Worcester sauce
Salt and pepper
1 Chopped red pepper
15-Ounce Can of drained kidney beans
Cooked Long-grain rice, to serve

DIRECTIONS

Fry the onion in a hot pan with oil until nearly brown then add chopped garlic
Add the mince and stir until brown; drain any excess fat if desired
Add all dried spices and seasoning then reduce heat and add chopped tomatoes
Stir well and add tomato purée and Worcestershire sauce then leave to simmer for about an hour.
Add the chopped red pepper and continue to simmer for 5 minutes, then add the can of drained kidney beans and cook for a further 5 minutes.
Serve with long-grain rice.

91. Vegan Rice Gumbo

Preparation Time: 5 minutes

Cooking Time: 25 minutes

Servings: 4

INGREDIENTS

4 large celery stalks

3 large carrots

1 medium onion

1 teaspoon dried thyme

1 teaspoon dried parsley

1 teaspoon garlic powder

1 teaspoon salt

1/2 teaspoon ground sage

1 tablespoon coconut aminos

4 cups vegetable broth

2 cups water

2/3 cup long-grain white rice

1 can of pinto beans

DIRECTIONS

Dice or chop the veggies into bite-size pieces.

Add a large pot to the stove and turn on medium heat. Spray the bottom of the pot with avocado oil or olive oil spray. Add veggies.

Cook the veggies for 3-4 minutes.

After 3-4 minutes, add spices, bay leaf, and coconut aminos. Stir and cook for 1-2 more minutes.

While veggies are cooking, rinse the rice well.

Add 1/2 cup of vegetable broth and scrape the bottom/side of the pot removing any brown bits from the bottom.

Add the rest of the broth, water, and rice to the pot. Stir and cover. Turn the heat up to high.

Once the Gumbo comes up to a boil, turn down the heat to low and cook for 15 minutes.

While the Gumbo is cooking, rinse and drain the beans. And add them to the Gumbo.

Right before serving, remove the bay leaves. Serve hot.

92. Bean and rice burritos

Servings: 10 servings

INGREDIENTS

1 can of Pinto beans

1 cup long-grain rice; cooked

½ cup Onions; frozen, chopped

½ cup peppers; frozen, chopped

½ cup Corn; frozen

Chili powder; dash

Lettuce, chopped

1 bunch of Scallions; chopped

Cumin; dash

Garlic powder; dash

¾ cup Water

Salsa, oil-free, low sodium

10 Tortillas, whole wheat

1 Tomato; chopped

DIRECTIONS

Sauté the frozen onions and green peppers in a few tablespoons of water in a skillet.

Drain and rinse the beans and place them in a skillet and mash with a potato masher. Add the cooked rice, corn, spices, and water. Heat 5 to 10 minutes until most of the water is absorbed, stirring occasionally.

Heat the tortillas quickly in a preheated skillet, a toaster oven, or a microwave.

Place a line of bean mixture down the middle of each tortilla, and add a teaspoon of salsa and any of the other toppings as desired.

Fold up ½ inch on each side, tuck in the top edge, and roll into a burrito. Serve immediately, topped with additional salsa if desired.

93. Rice and Bean Roll-Ups

Servings: 6

Preparation time: 20 minutes

Cooking Time: 55 minutes

INGREDIENTS

1 1/2 cups salsa

1 cup cooked long-grain rice

2 medium Roma tomatoes, chopped

1 small bell pepper, cut into 1/2-inch pieces

1 can of pinto beans, undrained

1 can whole kernel corn, drained

6 garden vegetable-flavored flour tortillas

1 cup shredded Mexican cheese blend

DIRECTIONS

Heat oven to 350°F. Spread 1/2 cup of the salsa in an ungreased rectangular baking dish, 13x9x2 inches.

Mix rice, tomatoes, bell pepper, beans, and corn. Spread about 1 cup of rice mixture on each tortilla; roll up the tortilla. Place seam sides down on salsa in the baking dish. Spoon the remaining 1 cup of salsa over tortillas. Sprinkle with cheese.

Cover and bake for 30 to 35 minutes or until heated through and cheese is melted.

For more spice, use the new jalapeño- or cilantro-flavored tortillas available in the supermarket.

94. Baked Pinto Bean Flautas with rice flour Tortilla

Preparation Time: 25 minutes

Cooking Time: 15 minutes

Servings: 25 flautas

INGREDIENTS

1/2 cup red onion

1/2 cup white onion

2 tablespoons avocado oil

1 large bell pepper diced

2 cups pinto beans

1.5 cups chickpeas

1 can of pinto beans, drained and rinsed

1/4-1/2 cup salsa verde

1 tablespoon chili powder

1 tablespoon garlic powder

1 tablespoons cumin

1/8 teaspoon cayenne pepper or paprika

1/8 teaspoon oregano

salt, to taste

2-3 tablespoons fresh chopped cilantro

2-4 cups of your favorite Mexican cheeses, shredded

25-30 small rice flour tortillas

DIRECTIONS

Preheat your oven to 385 degrees F.

Sauté your onion in a little bit of oil [2 tablespoons] to soften.

Next combine bell pepper, beans, and salsa in a large bowl.

Add onions to the mix and season with chili powder, garlic powder, cumin, cilantro, salt, cayenne, and oregano.

Next wrap a small stack of corn tortillas [4-5] in a damp paper towel and microwave on high for 30 seconds. Follow it up with an additional 30 seconds.

Once steamed, spray or rub one side of the tortilla with oil and add a thin layer of veggie filling vertically along the center of the opposite [un-oiled] of the tortilla. Top it off with a layer of cheese [as much or as little as you want!] and gently roll the tortilla.

tip: your steamed tortillas will naturally start to curl around each other in the stack. This is a total advantage since they naturally want to roll! When you unwrap your tortillas from the paper towel, oil the side facing up, and then put the filling on the side that is curling inwards. Viola!

Seal each flauta shut with two toothpicks and place on a wire baking/cooling rack. Repeat these steps until you have a rack full of flautas.

Place them on a wire rack on a foil-lined baking sheet. The wire rack elevates the flautas and allows them to get nice and crispy on both sides.

Sprinkle the finished product with a dash of, garlic powder and cayenne pepper.

Bake on the middle rack, at 385F, for approximately 15-18 minutes. At the very end, set the oven to broil on HIGH for just under a minute to crisp the tortillas into a perfectly golden, crunchy shell.

95. Rice and bean enchiladas with red sauce

Servings: 12 Servings

INGREDIENTS

12 9-inch flour tortillas; fat-free

FILLING

1 tablespoon Canola oil

2 Onions; chopped

6 cloves garlic; minced

16 ounces of Tomato sauce

1 tablespoon Chili powder

½ teaspoon Red pepper flakes; crushed

2 teaspoons ground cumin

2 teaspoons salt

5 cups cooked rice

3 pounds of Cooked beans

Water; as needed

⅔ cup Pitted black olives; chopped

8 ounces Sharp cheddar cheese; grated

½ bunch of Chopped cilantro leaves

DIRECTIONS

In a large non-stick sauté pan or sauce pan, heat oil. Add onion and garlic and cook until soft. Add tomato sauce, chili powder, pepper flakes, cumin, and salt. Cook slowly, uncovered, for 15 minutes to blend flavors.

Add half of the tomato mixture to the cooked beans in the bowl. Stir to blend. Add the cooked rice to the remaining half of the tomato mixture.

Preheat the oven to 350F.

Lightly oil a large baking dish. Place a thin layer of Red Sauce, on the bottom of the baking dish.

Dividing the filling 12 ways, place seasoned beans, seasoned rice, chopped olives, cheese, and cilantro on each tortilla.

Roll tightly and place, seam down, in a single layer in a baking dish.

Top with remaining Red Sauce. Cover with parchment or wax paper and top tightly with foil. Bake in preheated oven for 60 minutes. Remove foil and paper, sprinkle with 2 oz. of reserved cheese and bake an additional 15 minutes.

Serve with Fresh Green Salsa.

96. Rice and Bean Quesadillas

Total Time: 20 minutes

Servings: 4-6

INGREDIENTS

1 teaspoon olive oil-

1 cup cooked long-grain rice

15-ounce can of pinto beans, drained and rinsed

1 teaspoon cumin

1 teaspoon paprika

3/4 teaspoon garlic powder

1/2 teaspoon onion powder

4-6 tortillas

Sharp Cheddar Shredded cheese

DIRECTIONS

Heat a large pan over medium heat and add olive oil, rice, beans, and spices. Cook until heated through, about 3 minutes.

Lay your tortilla on a cutting board and sprinkle one half with a small handful of cheese 1/4 - 1/3 cup and then top with an equal amount of rice and bean mixture.

Fold tortilla over and place in a lightly greased pan. Cook quesadilla until cheese is melted and each side of the tortilla is golden brown, flipping once.

Let quesadillas cool for a few minutes before slicing.

97. Peruvian Tacu Tacu Cake

Total time: 35 minutes

SERVINGS: 2-4 servings

INGREDIENTS

FOR THE SALSA CRIOLLA

1/2 small red onion, thinly sliced

2 tablespoons chopped fresh cilantro leaves

2 tablespoons fresh lime juice

1/4 teaspoon aji Amarillo paste

1/4 teaspoon kosher salt

FOR THE TACU TACU

3 tablespoons grapeseed or safflower oil

1/2 small red onion, chopped

2 garlic cloves, chopped

1/2 teaspoon kosher salt, plus more to taste

1 teaspoon aji Amarillo paste

2 cups cooked or canned pinto beans, drained and rinsed

1 cup cold cooked long-grain white rice

1 tablespoon chopped fresh flat-leaf parsley leaves

1 tablespoon chopped fresh oregano

1 lime, cut into wedges

DIRECTIONS

Make the salsa: In a medium bowl, combine the onion with enough cold water to cover, and let sit for at least 10 minutes, then drain. Toss with the cilantro, lime juice, aji Amarillo and sal

Make the tacu tacu:

In a 10-inch nonstick skillet over medium-high heat, heat 1 tablespoon of the oil until shimmering. Stir in the onion and garlic and cook, stirring, until lightly browned, 5 to 6 minutes. Stir in the salt and aji Amarillo, and scrape the mixture into the bowl of a food processor. Wipe out the skillet.

Add 1 cup of the beans to the food processor and purée briefly until mostly smooth but still chunky. Scrape the mixture into a large bowl.

Add the remaining 1 cup of beans, the rice, parsley, and oregano to the bowl and stir to thoroughly combine. Taste, and add more salt if needed.

Return the skillet to medium heat and pour in another 1 tablespoon of oil. Add the rice-and-bean mixture and use a spatula to spread it around evenly and lightly pack it down.

Cook until deeply browned on the bottom, about 7 minutes. Remove from the heat, invert a plate on top of the skillet, and carefully flip both over to land the bean-and-rice cake bottom-side up onto the plate.

Return the skillet to medium heat, pour in the remaining 1 tablespoon of oil, and slide the cake back into the skillet.

Cook for another 7 minutes, or until deeply browned on the other side, then invert the plate and flip the skillet over again to land the cake onto the plate.

Top with the salsa and serve hot with lime wedges.

98. Alkaline Stew Peas with Dumplings

Total Time: 40 minutes

Servings: 4

INGREDIENTS

1 cup dried pinto beans, soaked overnight

1 onion, large

1 carrot, large

3 garlic cloves

1 stalk scallion

1 teaspoon thyme

½ teaspoon allspice, ground

1 tablespoon all-purpose seasoning

salt and pepper, to taste

1 scotch bonnet pepper, whole

1 cup coconut milk

1 tablespoons oil

DUMPLINGS

1½ tablespoons. white rice flour

1½ tablespoons. buckwheat flour

1 tablespoon potato starch

½ tablespoons tapioca flour

1 tablespoon almond flour

¼ teaspoon salt

2 tablespoons. water

DIRECTIONS

Drain soaked beans and place them in a pressure cooker. Cover with fresh water, about an inch above the beans. Cover and cook for about 20 to 25 minutes.

Meanwhile, chop the onion, garlic, carrot, and scallion then place them in a bowl.

In another bowl, combine all the dry Ingredients to make the dumplings. Gradually add water, mixing after each pour, until a firm dough starts to form.

Divide the dough into about 8 to 10 smaller pieces. Roll each piece between the palms of your hands in the shape of 3-inch long ropes or about the size of your pinkie finger. Set dumplings aside on a plate.

Once the beans are cooked, allow the pressure cooker to release pressure before opening. You can run the pot under cool tap water to help.

Remove the lid and add the chopped seasonings and remaining spices.

Add the coconut milk, and dumplings and simmer on low heat for 10 minutes.

Add the dumplings then cook for an additional 5 minutes until the dumplings are fully cooked. If the stew is too thick, add more water as needed.

Remove from heat. Serve with rice and steamed veggies or avocado.

99. Okra Curry

INGREDIENTS

250g okra (ladies finger) - cut into one cm pieces

2 Tablespoon grated ginger

1 Tablespoon mustard seeds

1/2 Tablespoon cumin seeds

2 Tablespoon oil

Salt to taste

Pinch asafetida

2-3 Tablespoon roasted peanut powder

Coriander leaves

DIRECTIONS

Heat the oil and add the mustard seeds. When they pop add cumin, asafetida and ginger. Cook for 30 seconds.

Add the okra and salt and stir until cooked. Add the peanut powder, cook for another 30 seconds.

Serve with coriander leaves.

100. Vegetable Coconut Curry

INGREDIENTS

2 medium sized potatoes, cut in cubes
1 1/2 cups cauliflower - cut into florets
3 tomatoes r chopped in large pieces
1 Tablespoon oil
1 Tablespoon mustard seeds
1 Tablespoon cumin seeds
5-6 curry leaves
Pinch turmeric - optional
1 Tablespoon grated ginger
Fresh coriander leaves
Salt to taste
Fresh or dried coconut - shredded

DIRECTIONS

Heat the oil then add the mustard seeds. When they pop add the remaining spices and cook for 30 seconds.
Add the cauliflower, tomato and potato plus a little water, cover and simmer, stirring occasionally until cooked. There should be some liquid remaining. If you want a dry curry, then fry for a few minutes until the water has evaporated.
Add coconut, salt and coriander leaves.

●

CONCLUSION

In New Orleans's early days, a gumbo was likely served as the first course of a meal. Today, given our fast-paced lives, a gumbo usually counts as the entrée on home tables. Restaurants are more likely to follow the old-school style with gumbo as an appetizer.

During the era of slave trading, okra was introduced to New Orleans by Africans, who, most food experts believe, brought the plant to southern plantations via the Caribbean. It was called gombo or kingombo in Bantu languages and was either boiled, fried, steamed, or pickled and served as both a thickener and a tasty ingredient that pairs well with seafood in gumbos.

Today, the meaning of "gumbo" goes beyond the culinary. Most any mixture might be called a gumbo—a political gumbo, a breed of dog, a fashion craze. It is a popular name for animals; one in particular was a St. Bernard and mascot of the New Orleans Saints in its early years.

Of all the dishes served in the melting pot, or gumbo, that is south Louisiana, this pungent, one-pot dish has become synonymous with the territory. Say "New Orleans," and we think "food" or we think "gumbo."

CPSIA information can be obtained
at www.ICGtesting.com
Printed in the USA
LVHW060706201222
735554LV00007BA/296

9 781805 422815